BASICS

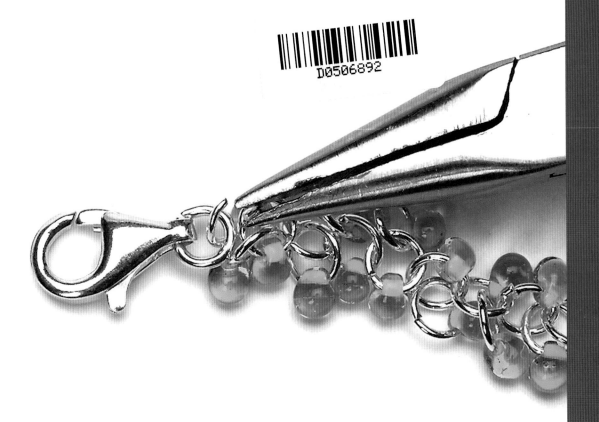

Choosing the right beads and the right tools to complete a project can be a challenge, but once you learn the basics, you'll be in good shape. Get started with seed beads by learning about different sizes, shapes, colors, and finishes. We'll guide you through the basics of needles, thread, and other tools and materials and teach you the basic beading skills you'll need to get started: knots, crimps, loops, and a wide range of stitches. We'll review some innovative ways to include seed beads in your bead-stringing projects, and then you will be ready to start exploring all the possibilities that seed beads provide.

SEED BEADS

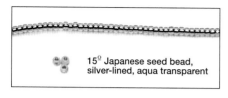
15º Japanese seed bead, silver-lined, aqua transparent

13º Czech Charlotte, copper-plated

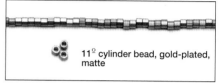
11º Czech 3-cut, black opaque

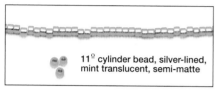
11º cylinder bead, silver-lined, mint translucent, semi-matte

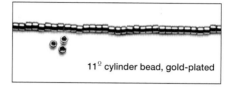
11º cylinder bead, gold-plated

11º cylinder bead, gold-plated, matte

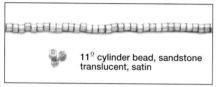
11º cylinder bead, sandstone translucent, satin

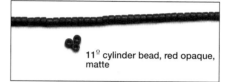
11º cylinder bead, red opaque, matte

11º Czech seed bead, silver, galvanized

11º Czech seed bead, light blue opaque, pearlized

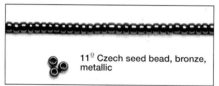
11º Czech seed bead, bronze, metallic

8º Czech seed bead, light peach transparent

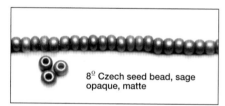
8º Czech seed bead, sage opaque, matte

6º Czech seed bead, copper-lined transparent

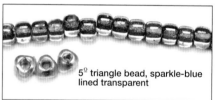
5º triangle bead, sparkle-blue lined transparent

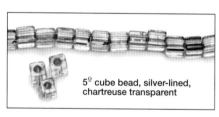
5º cube bead, silver-lined, chartreuse transparent

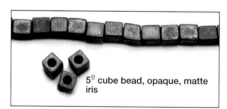
5º cube bead, opaque, matte iris

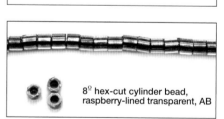
8º hex-cut cylinder bead, raspberry-lined transparent, AB

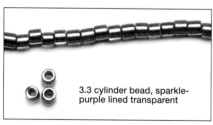
3.3 cylinder bead, sparkle-purple lined transparent

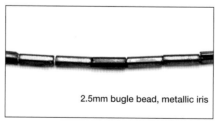
2.5mm bugle bead, metallic iris

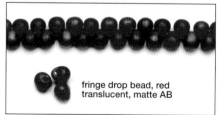
fringe drop bead, red translucent, matte AB

Seed beads come in packages, tubes, and hanks. A standard hank (a looped bundle of beads strung on thread) contains twelve 20-in. (51cm) strands, but vintage hanks are usually much smaller. Tubes and packages are usually measured in grams and vary in size.

Seed beads have been manufactured in many **sizes** ranging from the largest, 5º (also called E beads), which are about 5mm wide, to tiny size 20º or 22º, which aren't much larger than grains of sand. (The symbol º stands for aught or zero. The greater the number of aughts, i.e., 22º, the smaller the bead.) Beads smaller than Japanese 15ºs have not been produced for the past 100 years, but vintage beads can be found in limited sizes and colors. The most commonly available size in the widest range of colors is 11º.

Most round seed beads are made in Japan and the Czech Republic. **Czech seed beads** are slightly irregular and rounder than **Japanese seed beads**, which are uniform in size and a bit squared off. Czech beads give a bumpier surface when woven, but they reflect light at a wider range of angles. Japanese seed beads produce a uniform surface and texture.

Japanese and Czech seed beads can be used together, but a Japanese seed bead is slightly larger than the same size Czech seed bead.

Seed beads also come in a sparkly cut version. Japanese **hex-cut** or hex beads are formed with six sides. **2-** or **3-cut** Czech beads are less regular. **Charlottes** have an irregular facet cut on one side of the bead.

A new kind of seed bead was invented in the late 1980s by Mr. Masayoshi Katsuoka of Miyuki Shoji Co. The generic term for this bead is **Japanese cylinder bead**, otherwise known as Delica (the Miyuki brand name), or Toho Treasures (the brand name of Toho and Matsuno). Toho also has developed Aiko beads, a line of precision-cut cylinder beads. Japanese cylinder beads come in hundreds of colors and finishes, including gold- and silver-plated. Cylinder beads are extremely popular for peyote-stitch projects, such as amulet purses. These beads are very regular and have extremely large holes, which are useful for stitches requiring multiple thread passes. The beads fit together almost seamlessly, producing a smooth, fabric-like surface.

Cylinder beads usually are labeled size 11º, but they are about the size of a Czech 12º. In the mid '90s, Toho began making the 3.3 cylinder bead, so named because it is 3.3mm long. Miyuki calls its similar bead a size 8º Delica. Both sizes of cylinder beads (11º and 8º) are also available as hex-cuts.

Bugle beads are thin glass tubes. They can be sized by number or length. Size 1 bugles are about 2mm long, but bugles can be made even longer than 30mm. They can be faceted, hex-cut, straight, or twisted, but selection of colors, sizes, shapes, and finishes is limited.

Triangle beads have three sides. They are available in sizes 10º, 8º, and 5º. **Fringe drops** and **cube beads** are also a part of the seed bead family.

Seed beads are made with several types of glass: **opaque**, a solid-colored glass that light cannot pass through; **translucent**, a colored glass that light can pass through, but through which you can't see; and **transparent**, a clear or colored glass that you can see through. Transparent and translucent beads can be **lined** with colored glass or a colored, dyed, or painted lining. Silver- or gold-lined seed beads are lined with real silver or gold (silver-lined Czech beads usually have a square hole, which increases their sparkle).

Glass seed bead finishes can be **matte**, **semi-matte**, **satin**, or **shiny**, and may also be treated with a variety of coatings. These include **iris** or **aurora borealis (AB)**, which give multi-colored effects; **pearlized** (also called luster or ceylon); **metallic** (colored metal is fused to the glass surface); or **galvanized** (a rich but impermanent metallic coating). Some beads are **plated** with metals such as silver, gold, or copper. Many manufacturers and vendors recommend testing beads for colorfastness by subjecting them to normal usage tests – try rubbing the beads, washing them, and exposing them to sunlight.

CHOOSING SEED BEADS
People tend to favor one type of seed bead, but each type is better for some projects than for others. For example, to achieve a traditional Native American look, try opaque Czech seed beads. Today, Native American artists often use Japanese seed beads along with Czech beads in their non-traditional bead-work. In stitches where the beads meet each other end to end or side to side – peyote stitch, brick stitch, and square stitch – try Japanese cylinder beads to achieve a smooth, flat surface. For a more textured surface, use Czech or round Japanese seed beads. For right-angle weave, in which groups of four or more beads form circular stitches, the rounder the seed bead, the better; otherwise you risk having empty gaps or prevalent bead holes. Round seed beads are also better for netting and strung jewelry.

MATERIALS AND TOOLS

Selecting **beading thread and cord** is the single most important decision you'll make when planning a project. Review the descriptions below to evaluate which material is best for your design.

Threads come in many sizes and strengths. Size (diameter or thickness) is designated by a letter or number. OO and A/O are the thinnest, B, D, E, F, and FF are subsequently thicker. Cord is measured on a number scale; 0 corresponds in thickness to D, 1 equals E, 2 equals F, and 3 equals FF.

Parallel filament nylon, such as Nymo or C-Lon, is made from many thin nylon fibers that are extruded and heat set to form a single-ply thread. Parallel filament nylon is durable and easy to thread, but it can be prone to fraying and stretching. It is best used in beadweaving and bead embroidery.

Plied nylon thread, such as Silamide, is made from two or more nylon threads that are extruded, twisted together, and coated or bonded for further security. It is strong and durable and some brands have had the stretch removed. It is more resistant to fraying than parallel filament nylon. It's a good material for twisted fringe, bead crochet, and beadwork that needs a lot of body.

Plied gel-spun polyethylene (GSP) such as Power Pro or DandyLine is made from polyethylene fibers that have been spun into two or more threads that are braided together. It is almost unbreakable, it doesn't stretch, and it resists fraying. The thickness can make it difficult to make multiple passes through a bead. It is ideal for stitching with larger beads, such as pressed glass and crystals.

Parallel filament GSP, such as Fireline, is a single-ply thread made from spun and bonded polyethylene fibers. It's extremely strong, it doesn't stretch, and it resists fraying. However, crystals will cut through parallel filament GSP and it can leave a black residue on your hands and your beads. It's most appropriate for bead stitching.

Polyester thread, such as Gutterman, is made from polyester fibers that are spun into single yarns and then twisted into plied thread. It doesn't stretch and it comes in many colors, but it can become linty with use. It is best for bead crochet or bead embroidery when the thread must match the fabric.

Flexible beading wire is composed of wires twisted together and covered with nylon. This wire is stronger than thread and does not stretch; the higher the number of inner strands (between 3 and 49), the more flexible and kink-resistant the wire. It is available in a variety of sizes. Use .014 and .015 for most gemstones, crystals, and glass beads. Use thicker varieties, .018, .019, and .024, for heavy beads or nuggets. Use thinner wire, .010 and .012, for lightweight pieces and beads with very small holes, such as pearls.

Beading needles are coded according to size. Just like seed beads, the higher the number, the finer the beading needle. English beading needles are more flexible than Japanese needles. Unlike sewing needles, the eye of a beading needle is almost as narrow as its shaft. If you work with cylinder beads, you can use a thicker needle than is possible with Czech seed beads, which often don't accommodate a size #10 needle. As you become comfortable with seed beads, try using size #12 or #13 needles. These are harder to thread but easier to use than size #10s. Size #15 or #16 needles are often necessary when using vintage size 16°s or smaller beads. The number of times you will pass through the bead also affects the needle size that you will use. If you are using 11° seed beads, but you will be passing through them several times, you probably want to use a size #13 needle. For bead embroidery, you may prefer a short needle such as a size #12 between or #12 sharp.

Chainnose pliers have smooth, flat inner jaws, and the tips taper to a point. Use them for gripping and for opening and closing loops and rings.

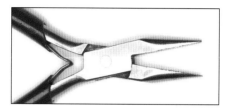

Roundnose pliers have smooth, tapered, conical jaws and are used to make loops. The closer to the tip you work, the smaller the loop will be.

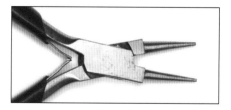

On **diagonal wire cutters**, the inside of the blades makes a pointed cut and the outside (back) of the blades meets squarely, yielding a flat-cut surface. Do not use your jewelry-grade wire cutters on memory wire, which is extremely hard; use heavy-duty cutters or bend it back and forth until it breaks.

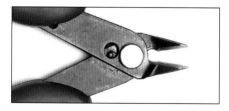

Crimping pliers have two grooves in their jaws that are used to fold or roll a crimp into a compact shape.

Split-ring pliers simplify opening split rings by inserting a curved jaw between the rings.

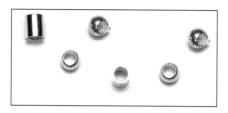

FINDINGS

A **head pin** looks like a blunt, long, thick sewing pin. It has a flat or decorative head on one end to keep the beads from falling off. Head pins come in different diameters, or gauges, and lengths.

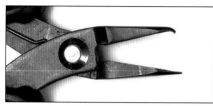

Eye pins are just like head pins except they have a round loop on one end, instead of a head. You can make eye pins from wire or head pins.

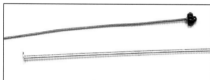

A **jump ring** is used to connect two loops. It is a small wire circle or oval that is either soldered or comes with a split that you can twist open and closed.

Split rings are used like jump rings but are much more secure. They look like tiny key rings and are made of springy wire.

Crimp beads are small, large-holed, thin-walled metal beads designed to be flattened or crimped into a tight roll. Use them when stringing jewelry on flexible beading wire.

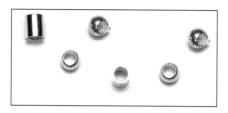

Clasps come in many sizes and shapes. Some of the most common are the toggle, consisting of a ring and a bar; the lobster claw, which opens when you push on a tiny lever; the S-hook, which links two soldered rings or split rings; the box, with a tab and a slot; and the tube, consisting of one tube that slides inside another.

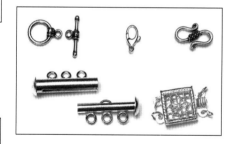

Earring wires come in a huge variety of metals and styles, including post, lever-back, French hook, and hoop. You will almost always want a loop (or loops) on earring findings so you can attach beads.

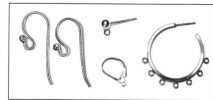

TECHNIQUES

Conditioning thread

Conditioning straightens and strengthens your thread and also helps it resist fraying, separating, and tangling. Pull unwaxed nylon threads like Nymo or C-Lon through either beeswax (not candle wax or paraffin) or Thread Heaven to condition. Beeswax adds tackiness that is useful if you want your beadwork to fit tightly. Thread Heaven adds a static charge that causes the thread to repel itself, so it can't be used with doubled thread. All nylon threads stretch, so maintain tension on the thread as you condition it.

KNOTS
Overhand knot

Make a loop and pass the working end through it. Pull the ends to tighten the knot.

Square knot

1 Cross the right-hand cord over the left-hand cord, and then bring it under the left-hand cord from back to front. Pull it up in front so both ends are facing upward.
2 Cross right over left, forming a loop, and go through the loop, again from back to front. Pull the ends to tighten the knot.

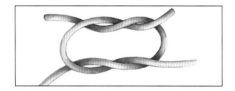

Surgeon's knot

Cross the left end over the right end and go through the loop. Go through again. Pull the ends to tighten. Cross the right end over the left end and go through once. Pull the ends to tighten.

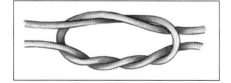

Half-hitch knot

Come out a bead and form a loop perpendicular to the thread between beads. Bring the needle under the thread away from the loop. Then go back over the thread and through the loop. Pull gently so the knot doesn't tighten prematurely.

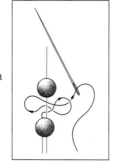

Front-back-front knot

1 Go through the loop on the clasp. Then thread one needle on each of the threads. Bring them back through the last bead.
2 Tie the first half of a square knot in front of the thread between beads.
3 Turn the strand over and tie the second half of a square knot on the other side of the thread. Turn the strand over once more and tie another half of a square knot in front of the thread. Run both needles through the next bead and make another front-back-front knot. Go through the third bead and make a final front-back-front knot. End by going through the fourth bead and trim.

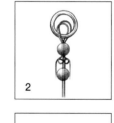

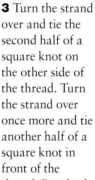

Larkshead knot

Fold a cord in half and lay it behind a ring, loop, bar, etc. with the fold pointing down. Bring the ends through the ring from back to front, then through the fold and tighten.

LOOPS AND JUMP RINGS
Plain loop

1 Trim the wire or head pin ³⁄₈ in. (1cm) above the top bead. Make a right-angle bend close to the bead.
2 Grab the wire's tip with roundnose pliers. The tip of the wire should be flush with the pliers. Roll the wire to form a half circle. Release the wire.

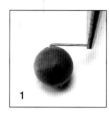

3 Reposition the pliers in the loop and continue rolling.
4 The finished loop should form a centered circle above the bead.

Wrapped loop

1 Make sure you have at least 1¼ in. (3.2cm) of wire above the bead. With the tip of your chainnose pliers, grasp the wire directly above the bead. Bend the wire (above the pliers) into a right angle.
2 Using roundnose pliers, position the jaws in the bend.

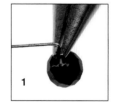

3 Bring the wire over the top jaw of the roundnose pliers.

4 Reposition the pliers' lower jaw snugly into the loop. Curve the wire downward around the bottom of the roundnose pliers. This is the first half of a wrapped loop.

5 Position the chainnose pliers' jaws across the loop.

6 Wrap the wire around the wire stem, covering the stem between the loop and the top bead. Trim the excess wire and press the cut end close to the wraps with chainnose pliers.

 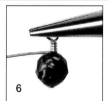

Opening and closing loops or jump rings

1 Hold the loop or jump ring with two pairs of chainnose pliers or chainnose and roundnose pliers, as shown.

2 To open the loop or jump ring, bring one pair of pliers toward you and push the other pair away. String materials on the open loop or jump ring. Reverse the steps to close the open loop or jump ring.

CRIMPS
Flattened crimp

1 Hold the crimp using the tip of your chainnose pliers. Squeeze the pliers firmly to flatten the crimp.

2 Tug the wire to make sure the crimp has a solid grip. If the wire slides, repeat the steps with a new crimp.

Folded crimp

1 Position the crimp bead in the notch closest to the crimping pliers' handle.

2 Separate the wires and firmly squeeze the crimp.

 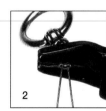

3 Move the crimp into the notch at the pliers' tip and hold the crimp as shown. Squeeze the crimp bead, folding it in half at the indentation.

4 Test that the folded crimp is secure.

STITCHING
Ladder

1 Pick up two beads. Leave a 4-in. (10cm) tail. Go through both beads again in the same direction. Pull the top bead down so the beads are side by side. The thread exits the bottom of the second bead (**a–b**). Pick up a third bead and go back through the second bead from top to bottom. Come back up the third bead (**b–c**).

String a fourth bead. Go through the third bead from bottom to top and the fourth bead from top to bottom. (**c–d**) Continue adding beads until you reach the desired length.

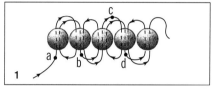

2 To stabilize the ladder, zigzag back through all the beads.

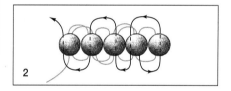

Brick stitch

Begin brick stitch with a ladder of seed or bugle beads (see "Ladder").

1 String two beads. Go under the thread between the second and third beads on the ladder from back to front. Pull tight. Go up the second bead added, then down the first. Come back up the second bead again.

2 For the row's remaining stitches, pick up one bead. Pass the needle under the next loop on the row below from back to front. Go back through the new bead.

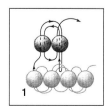 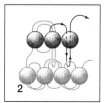

TECHNIQUES

Herringbone (Ndebele)

1 Stitch an even number of beads into a bead ladder (see "Ladder"). Turn the ladder, if necessary, so your thread exits the end bead pointing up. Pick up two beads and go down through the next bead on the ladder (**a–b**). Come up through the third bead on the ladder, pick up two beads, and go down through the fourth bead (**b–c**). Repeat across the ladder.

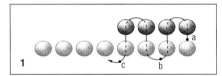

2 To turn, come back up through the second to last bead and continue through the last bead added in the previous row (**a–b**). Pick up two beads, go down through the next bead in that row, and come up through the next bead (**b–c**). Repeat across the row.

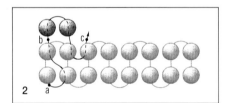

Peyote: flat even count

1 Pick up an even number of beads. These beads become rows 1 and 2.

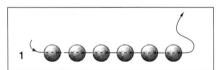

2 To begin row 3, pick up a bead and stitch through the second bead from the end. Pick up a bead and go through the fourth bead from the end. Continue across the row. End by going through the first bead picked up. To count rows, count the beads along the outer edges.

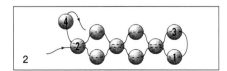

3 To start row 4 and all other rows, pick up a bead and go through the last bead added on the previous row.

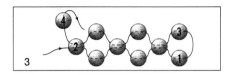

Peyote: flat odd-count

Work the first three rows as for flat, even peyote but string an odd number of beads. Since the first two rows total an odd number of beads, you won't have a place to attach the last bead on odd-numbered rows.

1 Work a figure-8 turn at the end of row 3, which will position you to start row 4: Pick up bead #7 and go diagonally through #2, then #1. Pick up #8 and go diagonally through #2, and #3. Turn, and go through #7, #2, and #1, then turn and go through #8 in the opposite direction. You can continue to work this turn at the end of each odd-numbered row, but this edge will be stiffer than the other. Use the following alternate method to turn on subsequent odd-numbered rows.

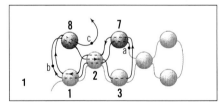

2 Pick up the last bead of the row, then go under the edge thread immediately below. Go through the last bead to begin the new row.

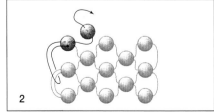

Peyote: gradual increase

1 The gradual increase takes four rows. At the point of the increase, pick up two thin beads. Go through the next high bead.

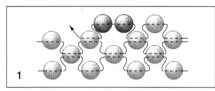

2 When you get to the two thin beads on row 2, go through them as if they were one bead.

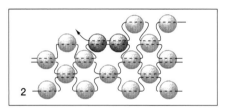

3 On row 3, place two regular-size beads in the two-thin-bead space.

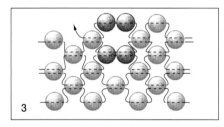

4 When you get to the two beads on the next row, go through the first, pick up a bead, and go through the second.

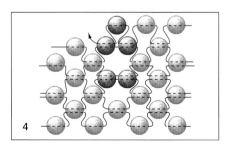

Peyote: gradual decrease

1 The gradual decrease takes four rows. At the point of the decrease, go through two high beads.

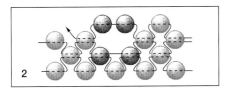

2 On the next row, at the point of the decrease, place in two thin beads in the space and go through the next high bead.

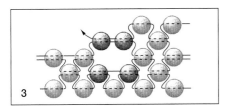

3 On row 3, go through the two added beads as if they were one bead.

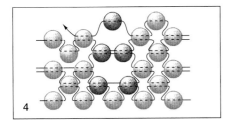

4 On row 4 at the decrease, pick up one bead and go through the next high bead.

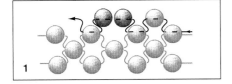

Peyote: rapid increase

1 At the point of the increase, pick up two beads instead of 1. Pass the needle through the next bead.

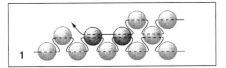

2 When you reach the double bead on the next row, go through the first bead, add a bead, and go through the second bead.

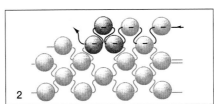

Peyote: rapid decrease

1 At the point of the decrease, don't pick up a bead. Instead, go through two beads on the previous row.

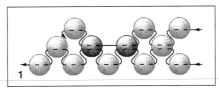

2 When you reach the point where you went through two beads, pick up one bead; continue peyote stitch.

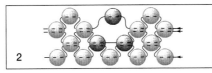

Peyote: tubular even-count

1 Pick up an even number of beads to equal the desired circumference. Tie the beads into a ring,

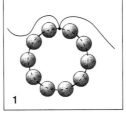

leaving some slack. Put the ring over a form, if desired.

2 Even-numbered beads form round 1; odd-numbered beads form round 2. Go through the first bead to the left of the knot. Pick up a bead, skip a

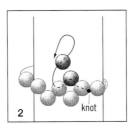

bead, and go through the next bead. Repeat until you're back at the start.

3 Since you started with an even number of beads, you need to work a "step up" to be in position

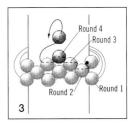

for the next round. Go through the first beads on rounds 2 and 3. Pick up a bead and go through the second bead on row 3; continue.

Peyote: tubular odd count

Start as for circular even-count steps 1–2 above. However, when you begin with an odd number of beads, there won't be a step up; you'll keep spiraling.

Peyote: two-drop

Work two-drop peyote stitch just like peyote stitch, but treat every pair of beads as if it were a single bead.

1 Start with an even number of beads divisible by four.

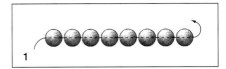

2 Pick up two beads, skip the first two beads, and go through the next two beads. Repeat across, ending by going through the last two beads.

TECHNIQUES

Peyote: zipping up (joining)

To join two sections of a flat peyote piece invisibly, fit the high beads on each side together, like the teeth of a zipper. "Zip up" the stitches by zig-zagging through each high bead.

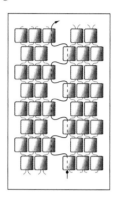

Right-angle weave

1 To start the first row, pick up four beads, and tie into a ring. Go through the first three beads again.

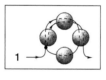

2 Pick up three beads. Go back through the last bead of the previous ring (**a–b**) and continue through the first two picked up for this stitch (**b–c**).

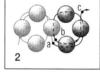

3 Continue adding three beads for each stitch until the first row is the desired length. You are sewing rings in a figure 8 pattern, alternating direction with each stitch.

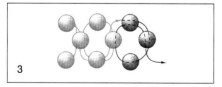

4 To begin row 2, go through the last three beads of the last stitch on row 1, exiting the bead at the edge of one long side.

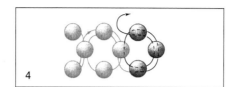

5 Pick up three beads, and go back through the bead you exited in the previous step (**a–b**). Continue through the first new bead (**b–c**).

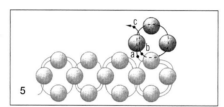

6 Pick up two beads, and go through the next top bead on the previous row and the bead you exited on the previous stitch (**a–b**). Continue through the two new beads and the next top bead of the previous row (**b–c**).

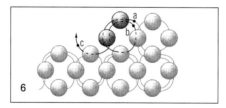

7 Pick up two beads, go through the bead you exited on the previous stitch, the top bead on the previous row, and the first new bead. Keep the thread moving in a figure 8. Pick up two beads per stitch for the rest of the row. When you go back through, don't sew straight lines across stitches.

Square stitch: single bead

1 String the required number of beads for the first row. Then string the first bead of the second row and go through the last bead of the first row and the first bead of the second row in the same direction. The new bead sits on top of the old bead and the holes are horizontal.

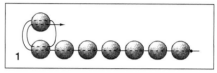

2 String the second bead of row 2 and go through the next-to-last bead of row 1. Continue through the new bead of row 2. Repeat this step for the entire row.

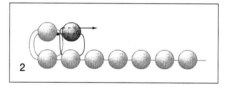

Stop bead

Use a stop bead to secure beads temporarily when you begin stitching. Choose a bead that is distinctly different from the beads in your project. String the stop bead about 6 in. (15cm) from the end of your thread, and go back through it in the same direction. If desired, go through it one more time for added security.

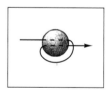

ADDING AND ENDING THREAD

To add, thread the needle on the tail end of the thread (where you cut it from the spool). Insert the needle in the bead where the old thread exits and go down four beads (**a–b** in the figure below). Go up three beads in the adjacent stack (**b–c**). Go down two beads in the first stack (**c–d**). Go up three beads in the second (**d–e**). Go down four to six beads in the third (**e–f**). Trim the short tail off and thread the needle on the long end. To end, follow a similar path to the way you added the new thread, working in the opposite direction.

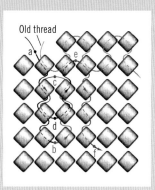

LOOMWORK
Set up the warp

Tie the end of the spool of thread to a screw or hook at the end of the loom.

Bring the thread over one spring and across to the spring at the other end of the loom. Wrap the thread around the back of the rod behind the bottom spring and back to the spring at the top of the loom.

Continue wrapping the thread between springs, keeping the threads a bead's width apart until you have one more warp thread than the number of beads in the width of the pattern. Keep the tension even, but not too tight. Secure the last warp thread to a hook or screw on the loom, then cut the thread from the spool.

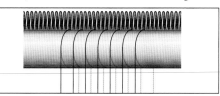

Weave the pattern

1 Tie the end of a 1-yd. (.9m) length of thread to the first warp thread just below the spring at the top of the loom. Bring the needle under the warp threads. String the first row of beads as shown on the pattern and slide them to the knot.

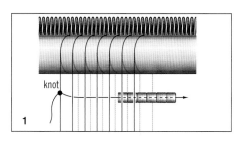

2 Push the beads up between the warp threads with your finger.

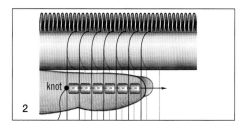

3 Sew back through the beads, keeping the needle above the warp threads. Repeat, following the pattern row by row.

Once you complete the last row, secure the working thread by weaving it into the beadwork.

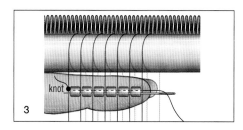

BEAD EMBROIDERY
Beaded backstitch

To stitch a line of beads, come up through the fabric from the wrong side. String three beads. Stretch the bead thread along the line where the beads will go, and go through the fabric right after the third bead. Come up through the fabric between the second and third beads and go through the third bead again. String three more beads and repeat. For a tighter stitch, string only two beads at a time.

Whipstitch

Whipstitch is a method of hand-sewing seams. Bring the needle through the material on the bottom side of the opening, and push it through the material on the upper side of the opening at an angle as shown. Repeat until the opening has been closed.

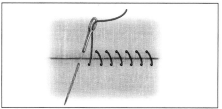

APPLICATIONS

Seed beads can be woven together to create complex patterns and textures. They also can be used to stitch intricate fabrics, ropes, and chains. Keep in mind, though, that seed beads lend themselves to simple projects as well. Their small size and wide range of colors and finishes make them ideal for use in easy stringing projects. Displayed here are several stunning pieces created with gemstones, pearls, crystals, and various types of seed beads.

Highlight a pendant by stringing seed beads in one or more strands, monochromatic or multicolored, in one or more sizes. The necklace above, designed by Karin Buckingham, uses two strands of seed beads in different colors and sizes with a cluster of crystals and pearls as the centerpiece.

Stringing sections of seed beads between groupings of gems, pearls, and other beads can make the larger beads stand out more effectively than they would if the necklace was made only with gems. In the citrine and peridot necklace (above, right), Sarah Ladiges included two or three colors of gemstones in every grouping with matte citrine-colored seed beads separating the gemstones. Using subtly different finishes – sparkling gems and crystals with lustrous pearls

and seed beads – adds visual texture, making the design more interesting than if all the beads shared a common texture.

Seed beads also make great, colorful spacers. In the summery necklace below, Julia Gerlach used size 11° seed beads to space 9mm blue quartz and 10 x 16mm lampworked beads. Using seed beads in a contrasting color sets off the focal beads and emphasizes the colorful nature of the necklace.

Seed beads are available in so many shades, sizes, and finishes, they provide near limitless opportunities for creative designs. Whether you're subtly blending colors or reveling in bold contrast, seed beads provide the perfect palette. A pre-mixed blend simplifies the design process, or you can meticulously select precise shades. This versatility in color options means fabulous results using very simple techniques.

Color blend collar

Seed beads of different colors and finishes combine to form this gradated necklace that shifts subtly from dark to light and back again.

by **Lesley Weiss**

String the gradations

[1] Cut ten 20-in. (51cm) lengths of flexible beading wire.

[2] Begin stringing the first strand, following the color gradations below:

Gradation 1: String nine color A beads, one color B, eight As, one B, seven As, one B, six As, one B, five As, one B, four As, one B, three As, one B, two As, one B, one A, two Bs, one A, three Bs, one A, four Bs, one A, five Bs, one A, six Bs, one A, seven Bs, one A, and eight Bs (**photo a**).

Gradation 2: String one color C bead, six Bs, one C, five Bs, one C, four Bs, one C, three Bs, one C, two Bs, one C, one B, two Cs, one B, three Cs, one B, four Cs, one B, five Cs, one B, six Cs, one B, and seven Cs.

Gradation 3: String one D, six Cs, one D, five Cs, one D, four Cs, one D, three Cs, one D, two Cs, one D, one C, two Ds, one C, three Ds, one C, four Ds, one C, five Ds, one C, and six Ds.

Gradation 4: String one E, six Ds, one E, five Ds, one E, four Ds, one E, three Ds, and one E.

[3] String two Ds, and then reverse the pattern (**photo b**), stringing all the color gradations in reverse to form a

a

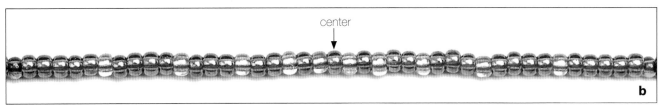

center

b

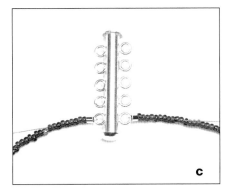

c

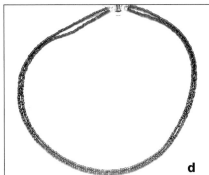

d

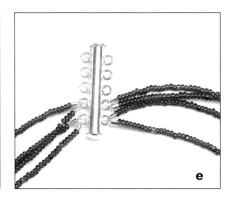

e

mirror image of the first half of the strand. Tape the ends to temporarily secure your beadwork.

[4] Repeat steps 2 and 3 to string nine additional strands.

Assemble the necklace

[1] Choose one strand to be the shortest strand. Close the clasp. Untape one end, and string a crimp bead and one end loop of the clasp. Go back through the crimp bead and a few seed beads. Repeat on the other end of the wire using the corresponding loop on the remaining clasp half (photo c). Gently tighten the wires, check the fit, and add or remove beads from each end, if needed. Crimp the crimp beads (see Techniques, p. 10), and trim the excess wire.

[2] Lay the necklace flat on your work surface, and align the center of the next strand with the first. Add beads to each end of the strand, if necessary,

to contour the second strand outside the first. Repeat step 1 to finish the second strand (photo d).

[3] Add a second pair of strands to the necklace as in steps 1 and 2, using the second loop on each clasp half (photo e).

[4] Repeat with the remaining strands, adding two strands to each loop on the clasp for a total of ten strands.

EDITOR'S NOTE: Choose your beads carefully and be sure to look at them in different lights. Remember – beads you buy in a tube or on a hank might look very different when strung on flexible beading wire.

MATERIALS
necklace 15¼ in. (38.7cm)
- 7g size 11º seed beads in each of **5** colors:
  silver-lined royal blue, color A
  Montana blue, color B
  denim blue, color C
  metallic steel blue, color D
  transparent color-lined sea blue, color E
- 5-strand tube clasp
- **20** crimp beads
- flexible beading wire, .010–.012
- crimping pliers
- wire cutters

COLOR

Play on color

Use a lively palette of seed beads to complement candy-colored lampwork beads.

by **Carol Pulk**

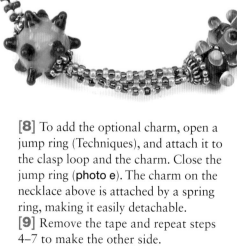

Necklace

You may substitute up to three small lampwork beads for one large bead. Or use other colorful beads instead of lampwork beads.

[1] Cut three 26-in. (66cm) lengths of flexible beading wire. Lay the wires together.

[2] String a bead cap, a lampwork bead, and a bead cap on the three wires.

[3] Center the beads and tape one side close to the beads (photo a).

[4] On the untaped side, string 20 seed beads on each wire, alternating the colors (photo b).

[5] Repeat steps 2 and 4 five times.

[6] String a spacer, a triangle or square bead, a spacer, a crimp, and a clasp half over all three wires. Go back through the crimp and the next few beads, tightening the wire to form a small loop (photo c).

[7] Crimp the crimp bead (see Techniques, p. 10), then trim the excess wire (photo d).

[8] To add the optional charm, open a jump ring (Techniques), and attach it to the clasp loop and the charm. Close the jump ring (photo e). The charm on the necklace above is attached by a spring ring, making it easily detachable.

[9] Remove the tape and repeat steps 4–7 to make the other side.

Bracelet

[1] Cut three 12-in. (30cm) lengths of flexible beading wire.

[2] Repeat steps 2 and 3 of the necklace.

[3] String eight seed beads on each wire, alternating the colors (photo f), then a bead cap, a lampwork bead, and a bead cap (photo g).

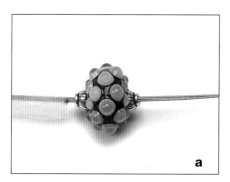

a

b

c

d

e

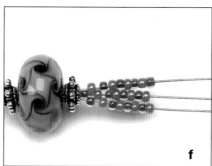

f

g

h

MATERIALS

both projects
- crimping pliers
- chainnose pliers
- wire cutters

necklace 21½ in. (54.6cm)
- **11** 8–15mm lampwork beads
- 2g size 11º seed beads in each of **12–24** colors
- **2** size 6º triangle beads or 5mm square beads
- **22** 4–8mm bead caps
- **4** 5mm spacer beads
- flexible beading wire, .010–.012
- toggle clasp
- charm (optional)
- 6mm jump ring or spring ring (optional)
- **2** crimp beads

bracelet 8 in. (20cm)
- **7** 8–15mm lampwork beads
- 2g size 11º seed beads in each of **6–12** colors
- **2** size 6º seed beads
- **10** 4–8mm bead caps
- **4** 5mm spacer beads
- flexible beading wire, .010 or .012
- clasp and 6mm soldered jump ring
- **2** crimp beads

[**4**] Repeat step 3 twice, but use spacers instead of bead caps on the last repeat.
[**5**] String a size 6º seed bead, a crimp bead, and the clasp. Go back through the crimp bead and the next few beads. Tighten the wire, then crimp the crimp bead (**photo h**). Trim the excess wire.
[**6**] Repeat steps 3–5 on the other end of the bracelet, but string a jump ring instead of the clasp.

EDITOR'S NOTE: Test your seed bead choices by stringing beads of alternating colors between two lampwork beads. To reduce the number of seed bead colors, limit your color choices but pair them differently.

Imitating gemstones

Simulate the richness
of gemstones by imitating
the colors of tourmaline
with seed beads.
Transparent beads in a
range of shades are ideal
for this gemstone effect.

by **Gloria Harris**

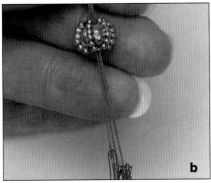

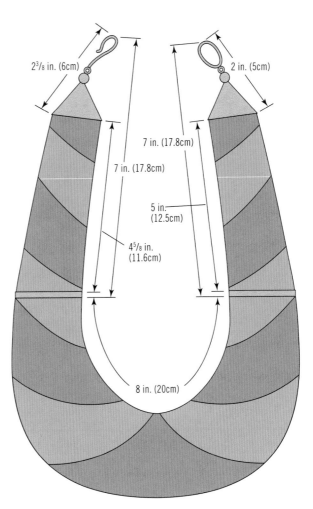

2³/₈ in. (6cm)

2 in. (5cm)

7 in. (17.8cm)

7 in. (17.8cm)

5 in. (12.5cm)

4⁵/₈ in. (11.6cm)

8 in. (20cm)

COLOR

MATERIALS

necklace 22 in. (56cm)

- 2 7-strand triangular spreaders
- 2 7-strand spacer bars
- 7g size 8º seed beads in each of 6–8 colors (3–4 graduated shades of green and 3–4 graduated shades of pink)
- Fireline, 10–12-lb. test
- large hook-and-eye or toggle clasp
- 2 10mm accent beads
- 7 twisted wire beading needles
- wire cutters
- G-S Hypo Cement

Getting started

[1] Cut seven 2-yd. (1.8m) lengths of Fireline. Gather them into a bundle. Fold the bundle in half, and pass the fold through the loop on one clasp half from front to back (photo a). Pull all the ends through the loop at the fold to make a larkshead knot (see Techniques, p. 10).

[2] Separate the strands of Fireline into pairs, and thread a twisted wire beading needle on each pair. String a 10mm bead over all seven pairs (photo b).

[3] One at a time, pass each needle through the single hole at the top of a triangular spreader and one of the bottom holes (photo c). You should have two strands of Fireline (one needle) exiting each hole.

Planning the necklace

Determine the finished length of your necklace. (This necklace is 22 in./ 53cm long at the shortest strand and 7 in./18cm long from the center of the clasp to the first spacer bar.) Subtract the length of half the clasp, one triangle, and the accent bead (2–2³/₈ in./5–6cm) from the length to the spacer bar. You'll string the remaining length – about 5 in. (13cm), on the inside strand and a bead or two more on each subsequent strand toward the outside to ensure that the spacer bar sits horizontally. The shortest front section of beads will be about 8 in. (20cm) long (figure).

The color order in this necklace was modeled after a blue and yellow sapphire necklace in Lois Sherr Dubin's *The History of Beads* (Abrams, 1987,

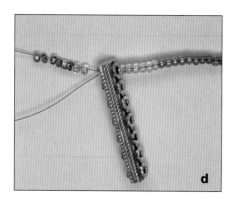

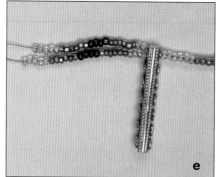

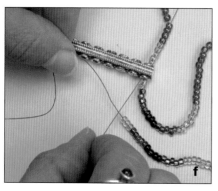

p. 189). Each color section begins and ends with the lightest tone graded to the darkest tone at the center of the section, and each strand becomes longer as you work toward the outer strands, as shown in the **figure**. It's important that color sections be continuous on each side of the spacer bars so that the bars serve as spreaders rather than dividers. Setting the color sections so that they fan out diagonally from the center of the necklace also makes the necklace look graceful rather than giving the impression of horizontal stripes. Do not line the colors up perfectly. This way the necklace will look more like natural gemstones.

Stringing the necklace

Lay the necklace flat to string it, and align each subsequent strand against the previous one. There are four pink colors and three greens, so the pink sections are slightly longer than the green ones. As you string, you'll find that the color groups don't angle perfectly, no matter how careful you are.

[1] On the innermost needle, string lightest to darkest to lightest pink for about 1 in. (2.5cm). Then string lightest to darkest to lightest green for about 1¾ in. (4.4cm). String a pink

section of about 2 in. (5cm) Then start a green section, and string through the inner edge hole of a spacer bar when you reach the desired length of beads (about 5 in./13cm on the right-hand side of the necklace).

[2] Remove one of the two threads from the needle, and thread it on a second needle. Finish the inside strand green section (**photo d**). Then finish the new strand green section, extending the green beads one or two beads longer than the innermost strand (**photo e**).

[3] String a pink section on each of the two needles, keeping the strands in order and making the second one just a bit longer than the first. Then string a green section. Stop three beads from the exact center measurement and string one each: lightest, darkest, and lightest pink.

[4] String the other side of the necklace as the mirror image of the first. After going through the spacer bar, string the top on one needle, and take the other needle through the beads (**photo f**).

[5] String through the inner hole and the top hole on the triangle and go through the accent bead. Tape the threads together to keep them snug against the accent bead.

[6] After stringing the first strand pair, tape the necklace to your work surface.

Tape the triangles at an angle as they will lie when worn; align the spacer bars horizontally and at the same height. Tape them in place.

[7] Repeat the stringing pattern, following the figure, until you have 14 center strands and seven side strands on each half of the necklace.

[8] Remove the tape, string a 10mm accent bead over all 14 strands, and pull all the ends through the loop on the other clasp half. Make sure the beads are snug, and divide the threads in half. Tie a front-back-front knot (Techniques) above the accent bead (**photo g**). Take all the ends through the accent bead, and tie another front-back-front knot below it. Bring the ends back through the triangle in pairs and tie a front-back-front knot around the strand below each of the seven holes. String the threads back through two to five beads. Glue all the knots. Trim the tails.

Seed bead blends

Tubes of seed bead mixes are a tempting purchase, but what do you do with them? Here are two fun and easy options for using pre-mixed seed bead blends to create casual jewelry.

Lariat

by **Karin Buckingham**

[1] Determine the finished length of your necklace. (These necklaces are 42–56 in./1–1.4m.) Add 8 in. (20cm), and cut a piece of flexible beading wire to that length.

[2] String a crimp bead, a few seed beads, a 10mm bead, and a drop bead or seed bead. Skip the last bead, and go back through all the other beads (**photo a**). Tighten the wire, and crimp the crimp bead (see Techniques, p. 10). String a few seed beads over both wires, and trim the short tail.

[3] String a random pattern of seed beads (or alternate groups of beads in different colors and sizes) to 5 in. (13cm) from the end of the wire.

[4] String a crimp bead and enough seed beads to go around the 10mm bead from step 1, plus a few extra. Go back through the first three or four seed beads and the crimp bead (**photo b**). Tighten the wire, check that the loop will fit over the button, and crimp the crimp bead. Go through a few seed beads, and trim the tail.

a

b

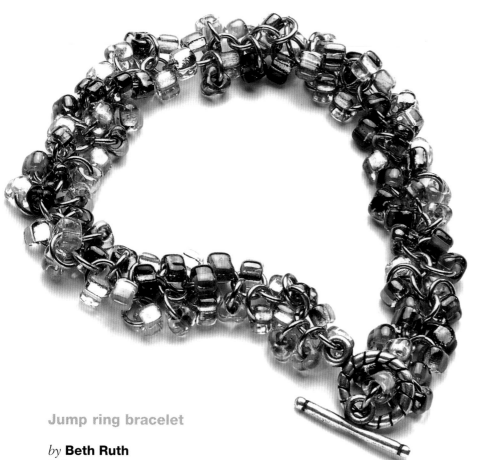

Jump ring bracelet

by **Beth Ruth**

[**1**] Using two pairs of pliers, open a jump ring (Techniques). Put one bead on the jump ring, and close the ring. Open another jump ring, and add a bead as before. Add this ring to the first jump ring, and close it (**photo a**).

[**2**] Continue adding beaded jump rings to the chain until you reach the desired length. (The chain portion of this 7½-in./19.1cm bracelet uses approximately 45 jump rings.) The rings on each end of the bracelet should touch when you wrap the chain around your wrist.

[**3**] To give the bracelet fullness, begin at one end and add a beaded jump ring to each ring along the chain.

[**4**] Use a jump ring to attach a lobster claw or half of a toggle clasp at one end of the bracelet (**photo b**). If using a toggle clasp, repeat on the other end with the second half of the clasp.

[**5**] If using a lobster claw clasp, you need to make an extension chain for the claw to grasp: At the end opposite the clasp, connect six plain jump rings. String six beaded jump rings on the end ring to create a decorative dangle (**photo c**). Close the jump ring.

MATERIALS

lariat 42–56 in. (1–1.4m)
- 15g seed bead mix
- 10mm bead
- **2** crimps
- flexible beading wire, .012
- crimping pliers
- wire cutters

bracelet 7½ in. (19.1cm)
- 10g size 6º seed beads, size 5º triangle beads, or tiny teardrop beads
- **100–110** 5mm jump rings
- lobster claw or toggle clasp
- **2** pairs of chainnose pliers

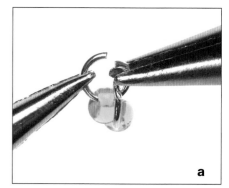

a

EDITOR'S NOTE: Both of these projects are easily converted from necklace to bracelet and vice versa. To wear the lariat as a bracelet, simply wrap it around your wrist and button it. To make a jump ring necklace, simply continue adding rings and beads until you reach the desired length.

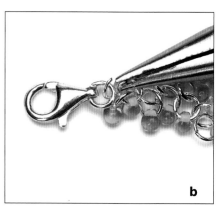

b

c

Techniques such as peyote stitch, loomweaving, square stitch, brick stitch or bead embroidery, combined with the multitude of bead colors available, allow you to virtually paint pictures with beads. Stitch these intricate patterns to make pendants, purses, or even wall hangings.

Reading a pattern

Render all sorts of images in beads by following stitch-specific patterns. Start with a simple pattern in a familiar stitch, and you'll soon find yourself tackling more challenging patterns, such as those shown here.

Hummingbird pattern by **Lila Tubbs**
Geometric tapestry pattern by
Jennifer Creasey

[1] Start by sorting the required beads by color. Make individual piles on your work surface, or fill small, flat dishes with each color. Label each color with a number or letter to match the color chart on your pattern, and arrange the beads in order (**photo a**).

[2] If you're working with a peyote pattern, the rows are offset to match the position of the beads. A guide makes it easier to follow the pattern. To make a guide, lay a piece of paper over your pattern, and trace the vertical lines that separate the beads onto the paper's edge. Using a ruler, draw the first and last vertical lines about ¼ in. (6mm) long. Connect the lines along the bottom. Cut each vertical line to the ¼-in. mark. Fold over every other strip, and tape the strips down (**photo b**).

If you're working a large pattern, laminate your guide for durability.

To use the guide, place it over the pattern, and pick up the beads that show between the strips (**photo c**).

[3] If you're following a pattern for loomwork or square stitch, the pattern rows form a grid. Simply place a ruler along the horizontal grid lines to help you keep your place.

[4] Start at one corner of the pattern, and pick up beads for the bottom row. (Remember that in peyote, the first beads you pick up become rows 1 and 2.) Work back and forth to stitch the subsequent rows.

[5] To end a thread, sew back through several rows, working through the beads until the thread feels tight and secure. Trim the tail.

To start a new thread, begin several rows away from where you want the new thread to exit, and work through the beads as before.

[6] To add hanging tabs, work the tabs in square or ladder stitch (see Techniques, p. 10). To add decorative points, work the pattern with peyote decreases (Techniques).

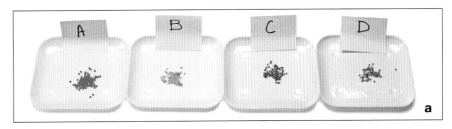

a

b

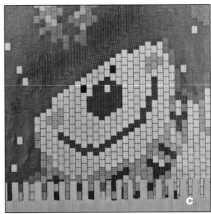

c

EDITOR'S NOTE: Most patterns for bead stitches and loomwork are designed for Japanese cylinder beads, which are uniform in size; if there's no mention of another bead type, you can assume that the pattern calls for cylinders. Cylinder beads are often referred to by their brand names: Delica beads by Miyuki, and Treasure and Aiko beads by Toho. With cylinder beads, use #10 or #12 beading needles and Nymo B (or an equivalent) thread. Condition the Nymo (Techniques) if desired.

Woven pendant

Adorn a loomed pendant with fringe.
If desired, add a cabochon and embellish
with bead embroidery.

by **Heidi Kummli**

The pattern

[1] Set up the loom with 26 warp threads (see Techniques, p. 10), which is one more warp thread than the number of beads across the width of the pattern.
[2] Start a 2-yd. (1.8m) weaving thread, or weft, and leave an 18 in. (46cm) tail. Weave part 1 of the pattern (Techniques).
[3] You need to decrease two times in part 2. To decrease, sew back through the beads you need to skip on the next row, and exit at **point a**. Wrap the weft around the warp thread as shown in **figure 1**. Now you are in position to start the next row. Repeat to make the second decrease at **point b**.
[4] End the weft by tying it to the warp thread next to the last bead on the last row. Then weave through a few beads, and trim the excess thread. Seal the knot with G-S Hypo Cement.

[5] To weave the bail (part 3 of the geometric pattern), thread a needle on the tail, and sew through the beads on row 1 to exit at **point c**. Wrap the weaving thread around the warp as you did in step 3, and weave the bail from the bottom up. For the flower pattern, exit at **point c**, weave the left strip, and end the thread. Start a new thread, exit at **point d**, and work the right section of the bail.
[6] Secure the weft, and trim.

Finish the warp threads

[1] While your piece is on the loom, tape the warp threads as shown (**photo a**). Don't tape the warp threads too close to the loomwork or the tape will show along the edges.
[2] Trim the warp threads just past the tape. Place the loomwork on a flat surface. Flatten the tape with the edge of a ruler to secure the threads.

[3] Trace the shape of the pendant, but not the bail, on poster board. Then cut out the shape, making it slightly smaller than the actual loomwork.
[4] Glue the poster board cutout to the back of the loomwork with tacky glue (**photo b**). Fold the warp threads over the poster board and glue the tape to the board. Let it dry under a heavy, flat object like a thick book to keep it flat.
[5] Fold the bail over so it forms a loop above the pendant, and glue the tape to the board (**photo c**). Allow the glue to dry, as before.

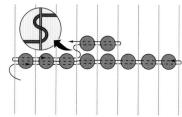

FIGURE 1

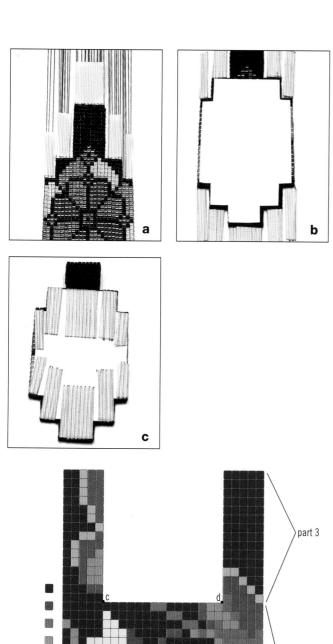

a

b

c

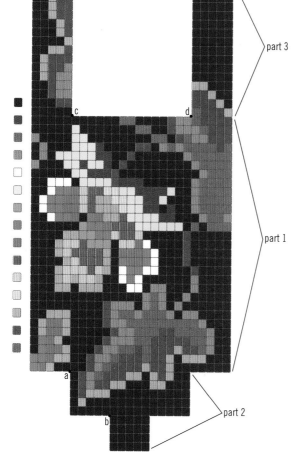

c   d

part 3

part 1

a

part 2

b

FLOWER PATTERN

part 3

d   c

part 1

a

b

part 2

GEOMETRIC PATTERN

Attach the cabochons

[1] Apply E6000 to the loomwork where you want to set the cabochon. Work the glue into the spaces between the beads with a toothpick. Apply glue to the back of the cab, set it in place on the loomwork, and let it dry.
[2] With a #12 sharp, make a hole in the board just above the cab.
[3] Thread the sharp with a 2-ft. (61cm) length of conditioned Nymo (Techniques) or Fireline, and knot the end. Sew through the hole from the back to the front of the loomwork.
[4] Pick up six 15º seed beads and position them along the edge of the cab. Sew through the loomwork and board next to the sixth 15º (photo d).
[5] Position the needle between the third and fourth 15º, and make a hole in the board, as in step 3. Sew through the board from the back to the front, and sew back through the last three 15ºs.
[6] Continue working in beaded back-stitch (Techniques) around the cab. Then sew through all the 15ºs again, and pull them snug against the cab. Work a second row if desired. Secure the thread, and trim.

Finish

[1] Cut a piece of Ultrasuede slightly larger than the loomwork.
[2] Glue the Ultrasuede to the board on the back of the loomwork with tacky glue. Press the loomwork flat against the Ultrasuede to smooth out the glue.
[3] After the glue is dry, carefully trim the Ultrasuede around the loomwork.
[4] Using the #12 sharp and a 1-yd. (.9m) length of thread, knot one end of the thread. Position your needle at

point d on the pattern, between the loomwork and the Ultrasuede. Sew through the Ultrasuede near the edge to hide the knot, and go under the thread bridge in the corner of the loomwork.
[5] Pick up four 15ºs, and sew under the thread bridge between the third and fourth beads on the loomwork. Sew through the Ultrasuede and up through the fourth 15º (photo e).
[6] Repeat step 5 around the pendant. As you work, adjust the number of 15ºs to follow the contour of the pendant.

Fringe

[1] Secure a 1-yd. length of thread in the Ultrasuede, as in step 4 of "Finish," where you will place the first strand of fringe.
[2] Pick up three to five 15ºs or 11ºs, a few accent beads, and three to five 15ºs or 11ºs. If adding a charm, sew through the loop on a charm, and pick up the same number of 15ºs or 11ºs. Sew through the accent beads (photo f). Pick up three to five 15ºs or 11ºs, and sew through the loomwork to the back of the pendant (photo g).
[3] Continue adding fringe as desired. Secure the thread, and trim.

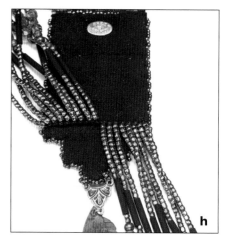

EDITOR'S NOTE:

Stitch long fringe (pendant, p. 30) to the edge of a piece of Ultrasuede that is slightly smaller than the pendant. Then glue it to the back of the pendant before you stitch the edging (photo h).

MATERIALS

pendant
- 1–2g size 11º Japanese seed beads, in each of 6–15 colors (see patterns, p. 31)
- 2–3g size 15º seed beads
- 6 x 8–10 x 14mm cabochon
- assorted accent beads and charms for fringe (optional)
- Ultrasuede
- Nymo B or Fireline, 6–8-lb. test
- beading needles, #12 and #12 sharp
- beading loom
- Aleene's Tacky Glue
- E6000 adhesive
- G-S Hypo Cement
- ¾ in. (1.9cm) masking tape
- poster board

Wildflower purse

Follow the wildflower peyote pattern to make a lovely purse. Embellish the image and add a textured strap and fringe.

by **Susan Hillyer**

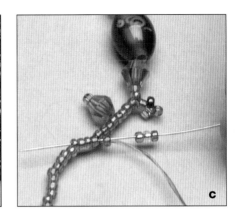

Make the bag

[1] First make a form with poster board and felt to stabilize the peyote work in progress. The tube should be 2⅜ in. (6cm) in diameter or 7¾ in. (19.7cm) circumference and 3½ in. (8.9cm) tall. Attach a circle of poster board to one end to support the tube. Cut six to eight graduated circles of felt to make a dome, and glue them to the end of the tube (**photo a**).

[2] Thread a needle with 2 yd. (1.8m) of conditioned Nymo (see Techniques, p. 10). Pick up 43 color A beads and one color B bead four times. These 176 beads will accommodate the flower design four times.

[3] Tie the strand of beads around the form with a square knot (Techniques). There should be a gap of about four to six beads. This gap will keep your beadwork supple. If there is not enough slack in the initial rows, the purse will be too rigid.

[4] Work six rows of tubular peyote (Techniques) with As. On the seventh row, stitch the top bead of each flower pattern in line with a marker bead. Follow the graph (**figure 1**) to complete the body of the bag. To finish or start a new thread, zigzag through several rows of beads to secure the end of the thread (Techniques).

[5] After you complete the graphed pattern, continue working with As. Begin to decrease (Techniques) as needed to keep your beadwork snug against the form until the bottom closes.

Embroider the flowers

[1] Secure a new 2-yd. length of conditioned Nymo and zigzag through several rows, exiting one of the purple flower beads.

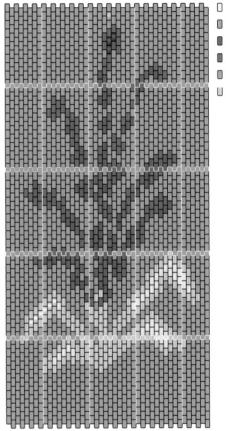

FIGURE 1

[2] Pick up one to three beads in a selection of purples and whites. Sew through one of the beads next to the bead you exited (**photo b**). Sew beads or bead clusters randomly over the top of each of the flower patterns. The more bead clusters you add, the more three-dimensional the flowers will appear.

Attach and embellish the strap

[1] Secure a new 2½-yd. (2.3m) length of Nymo near the bottom of the bag, and zigzag through the beadwork,

exiting an edge bead between two flowers. Pick up 2 in. (5cm) of As.

[2] Pick up a 4mm crystal, a 12mm accent bead, a crystal, 44 in. (1.1m) of As, a crystal, a 12mm, and a crystal. You can, of course, modify the strap length to suit your requirements.

[3] Pick up 2 in. of As, and sew into the edge beads directly opposite where your thread exited at the start of the strap. You should be entering a bead between two flower patterns. Zigzag far down into the rows of the purse to distribute the purse's weight, secure the tail with several half-hitch knots, and trim the tail.

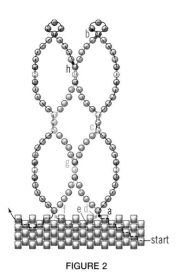

FIGURE 2

d

MATERIALS
purse
- size 15º seed beads:
  50g emerald green, color A
  20g each of **4** shades of purple,
  colors B–E
  20g each of **2** shades of white,
  colors F and G
  10g mint green, color H
  10g gold, color I
- **2** 12mm oblong glass beads
- **2** 8mm round glass beads
- **60–100** 4mm purple bicone crystals
- **60–100** 4mm amethyst rounds
- beading needles, #12
- Nymo B, conditioned with beeswax
- 10 in. (25cm) rattail cord
- poster board
- felt

[4] Secure a new 2½-yd. length of Nymo, zigzag through the purse, and exit the edge approximately 21 up-beads from where you began the strap. There should be a flower design between the two exit beads.

[5] String 2 in. of As, and sew through the crystal, 12mm, crystal, and the two As strung at the beginning of step 2.

[6] To embellish the strap, pick up any of the following bead groups:
- three or four seed beads in a variety of purples, greens, and whites.
- a 4mm crystal and a seed bead.
- a 4mm round and a seed bead.

[7] Sew back through the first bead on the fringe (the seed bead, the crystal, or the round), and go through the next four beads on the strand (**photo c**). Add an embellishment every four beads until you reach the crystal, 12mm, and crystal at the other end.

[8] Sew through the crystal, 12mm, and crystal, and string 2 in. of As. Enter the edge of the purse about 21 up-beads over from where the first strand is attached. Zigzag deep into the purse, secure the tails and trim.

[9] Secure a new 2½ yd. thread, and embellish one of the 2-in. sections of As. Add bead groups along the rest of the purse strap between the groups already added.

[10] Repeat step 9, embellishing until you are satisfied with the strap's

appearance. The more you embellish it, the more beautiful and sturdy the strap will be. If you come upon a bead that you can no longer sew through, string a few seed beads to make a bridge over that bead, and continue embellishing.

Fringe

This bag has 27 fringes, but you can do any number you choose. Each fringe is 2–5 in. (5–13cm) long. Make longer fringes toward the center and shorter ones on the periphery of the fringed area.

[1] Secure a 2-yd. length of Nymo. Zigzag through the bottom of the purse a few times, exiting close to the center.

[2] String 2–5 in. of As, a round bead, a bicone crystal, and another A. Skip the last bead, and sew back through the crystal and the round.

[3] Pick up three seed beads in a variety of purples, whites, and greens, and go through the next A.

[4] Repeat step 3, adding embellishments along the entire strand.

[5] After you finish embellishing the first fringe, sew through a few beads on the purse bottom. Repeat steps 2–4 to make as many fringes as you desire. Secure the tail, and trim.

Netted edge and drawstring

Keep the strap tucked inside the purse while making the netted edge.

[1] Secure 2 yd. of Nymo in the purse

by zigzagging through the beadwork. Exit an up-bead on the edge of the purse.

[2] Pick up five As, a B, an F, a B, four As, an H, an I, an H, four As, a B, an F, a B, four As, and four Bs.

[3] Sew back through the first B of the last group of Bs added (**figure 2, a–b**). Pick up four As, a B, an F, a B, and four As. Sew back through the H, I, and H beads (**b–c**).

[4] Pick up four As, a B, an F, a B, and four As. Sew through the first A of this strand (**c–d**). Sew into the next up-bead (**d–e**) and continue through the top edge, exiting two up-beads over from the bead you entered (**e–f**).

[5] Pick up five As and sew through the B, F, B group on the first loop of the netting (**f–g**).

[6] Pick up four As, an H, and I, an H, and four As. Sew through the B, F, B group on the second loop of the netting (**g–h**). Pick up four As and four Bs.

[7] Repeat steps 3–6 until the entire edge is netted. Secure the tail and trim.

[8] On each end of the rattail cord, sew a round 8mm bead. If you wish, embellish the end with a tube of circular peyote above the bead. Thread the rattail cord through the center loops on the netting (**photo d**).

Embroidered portrait

Transform a photo into fabulous bead embroidery. By developing a pattern and embroidering directly on the surface, you can recreate any image you desire in beads.

by **Siobhan Sullivan**

Select and size the image
[1] Pick a photo or print that is clear. A copyright-free professional portrait or photo is ideal.
[2] To begin sizing the image, pick the area in the image that is the most interesting to you. For instance, in the portrait of Eleanora de Toledo (at right), the focus is on her face. If you are using a computer, crop and size the image to print out at 4 x 6 in. (10 x 15cm). If you are using a color copier, copy the original image and cut away what you don't want. Then resize the part you do want to 4 x 6 in.
[3] When you are satisfied with your image, make three color copies; one for tracing, one for color reference, and one for marking up.

Transfer the image to fabric
A light-colored fabric is easiest to work with – the better you can see the holes, the faster the beading will go.
[1] Cut the fabric to 5 x 7 in. (13 x 18cm). Apply Fray Check around the edges of the fabric, and let it dry. This prevents the fabric from unraveling while you work on it.
[2] Lay the fabric on a hard flat surface, and tape it down at the corners. Make sure it is straight.
[3] Cut a piece of wax-free transfer paper, and center it ink-side-down on the fabric. Tape down the corners.
[4] Place your tracing copy with the image right-side up over the transfer paper and the fabric. Tape the tracing

copy in place. Using a sharp pencil or a ballpoint pen, trace over all the image's major features (**photo a**). Then draw a defined border all around the image. To check your tracing, lift the tracing copy and the tracing paper up from the bottom only, and retrace anything that is not clear enough. When you are done tracing, your fabric will look something like **photo b**.

Prepare the image
[1] Fill in the image with colored pencils, using your color reference copy as a guide. It's fine if the pencil colors don't match the original's colors. What is most important is to define the image's highlights and shadows. These light and dark areas are what make

an otherwise flat piece appear three-dimensional. Your colored fabric may look something like **photo c**.
[2] If the image you are using is a facial close-up like Eleanora de Toledo, there are a few simple tricks to make the face more interesting, even though these may not be obvious in the original:
• Make the middle of the forehead and cheekbones lighter than the rest of the skin.
• Give the hollows of the cheeks a slightly different color from the rest of the face.
• Choose a color that is a couple of shades darker than the rest of the skin for the skin at the hairline.
• Make sure that the nose casts a shadow.

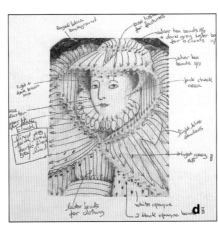

MATERIALS

portrait
- desired image, sized
- size 11º Japanese cylinder beads, assorted colors
- sewing thread (100% polyester)
- beading needles, #10 or #12
- beeswax
- Aida cross-stitch fabric, 16 count
- Fray Check seam sealer
- wax-free tracing paper
- threaders
- tape
- color copier
- colored pencils
- crimping pliers
- embroidery scissors
- fabric-cutting scissors
- pencil or ballpoint pen

optional extras
- size 15º seed beads
- size 11º seed beads
- faux or freshwater pearls
- faux or real gemstone beads
- lace
- trims
- vintage jewelry
- Beacon Fabri-Tac glue
- computer with graphics editing program and printer

PATTERNS

• Make slight shadows under the nose, eyes, and chin and over the brows. Make darker shadows under the brows.

• Choose a lighter color for the middle of the upper eyelid than for the rest of the lid.

• Make the lower lip slightly lighter than the upper lip.

• Use one white bead in the eye area to determine the direction of the subject's gaze. Look carefully at your original to determine its position.

[3] The markup copy (photo d) is your strategy tool. This is where you plan how you'll create movement, texture, and depth in the piece. You'll also plan any special effects you may want.

• Movement – Look at your image to determine the direction(s) of the objects in it. For example, in the Mary Queen of Scots piece on p. 38,

she has a billowing cloak that ties at the neck then falls over her clothes. Her bodice is pleated, and there is a blanket over her lap. Draw arrows on the paper to map out the directions the material flows. You'll be stitching the beads in these directions.

• Texture – Again using Mary Queen of Scots as an example, she is wearing ermine fur (white with black spots). Opaque white and black beads show the difference between the fur and the rest of her clothing. The opaque beads look a little rougher than the rest. Hex-cut beads or bugle beads might have worked as well.

• Depth – The use of highlight, midtone, and shadow areas creates depth. You'll already have some idea where these go after coloring your fabric. However, here is where you will make notes of specific beads you will use to produce those areas.

• Special effects – Mary Queen of Scots' cloak is made of a shiny translucent material. When it falls over the ermine, it tones down and shadows the fur's colors. In this piece, lined gray crystal beads were used for the ermine spots that show under the cloak. The spots are still visible, and the shine of the cloak is evident as well.

Bead the piece

[1] The following tips will help make the beading go smoothly:

• Always wax the thread well.

• Use a 2-ft. (61cm) maximum length of thread to avoid tangling.

• Keep the background simple, with all the beads facing the same direction.

• To remove small areas of beads, you can simply break each bead using crimping pliers. For larger areas, cut the beads and thread out carefully with sharp embroidery scissors.

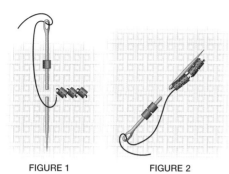

FIGURE 1   FIGURE 2

[2] Use tent stitch (**figure 1**) with the beads slanting from left to right. For plain or focal areas, like the face and background, sew one bead at a time and one horizontal row at a time.

[3] Hair, clothing, and jewelry are areas that add movement and texture. Use beaded backstitch (**figure 2** and Techniques) to sew the beads on in curved lines according to your markup. Continue stitching from one hole in the fabric to the next if you can.

Creating tight curves can be tricky. Sometimes the beads are too far apart or they bunch up. If the beads are far apart, backstitch back through the beads and add an extra bead into the line at the gap. If the beads are bunched up, use crimping pliers to break one or two of the beads in the curve until it lies flat.

Finish the piece

[1] When the image has been completed, trim the fabric, leaving at least ¼ in. (6mm) all around. Reseal the edges with Fray Check.

[2] Turn the ¼-in. edges under, and sew or glue the beadwork panel in place on your chosen material.

[3] If you want to conceal the edge of the fabric, use some type of trimming such as cloth, ribbon, or a fabric paint that matches your chosen mounting material.

[4] Finally, add embellishments as desired. Wherever possible, sew them on, especially if the piece is going to be used regularly (like a handbag). If you use glue, never use Crazy Glue or any other type of cyanoacrylate glue. It does not hold, and it will destroy your beads and thread. Use a good fabric gel-type glue, such as Beacon Fabri-Tac, which can also be used to mount your piece to a backing.

EDITOR'S NOTE: This type of project is not an exact science. You may change colors, leave out what you don't want, or add to the design. Don't try to duplicate every detail because you can't. Instead, focus more on the overall feel. If you don't like the way something looks, you can always redo it. This is your project, so remember to have fun.

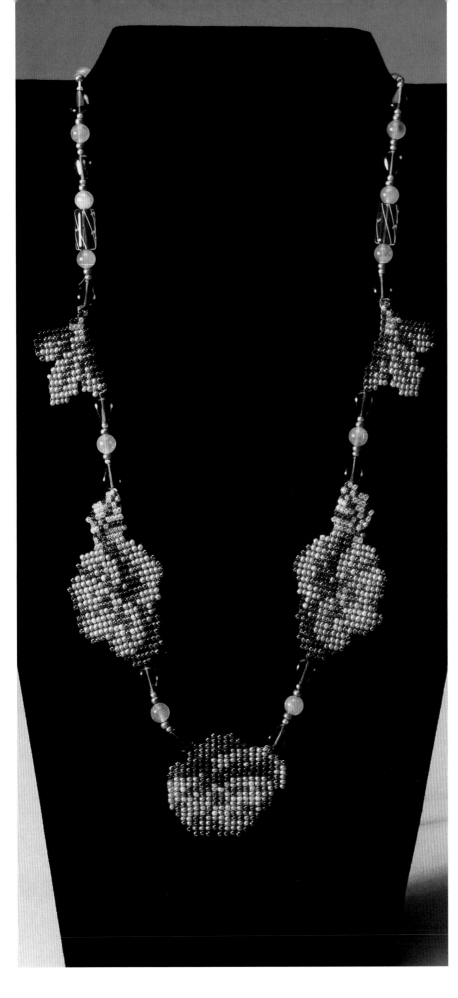

Patterned pansies

Stitch up these purple pansies for a delightful springtime accessory. Learn increases and decreases in horizontal square stitch to achieve unusual shaping.

by **Rebecca Starry**

Horizontal square stitch begins much like herringbone stitch, but has an extra thread pass to pull the beads into the classic square stitch alignment. When following charted patterns, it's sometimes easier to lay out the beads in order for each row as you come to it before sewing them in place. To keep your place on a charted pattern, try using Note Tape. It doesn't mark up the pattern and is easy to move from one row to the next.

After working pansy #1, you can finish it as a brooch or make a second one for a pair of earrings. For the necklace, you'll need one pansy #1, two pansy #2s, and two pansy #3s. After you understand how to work horizontal square stitch, feel free to design your own flowers or other images on square-grid graph paper. Or, use a grid designed for loomwork with Czech seed beads, but turn it 90

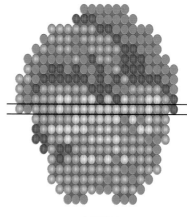

PANSY 1

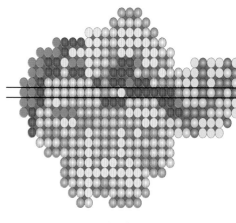

PANSY 2

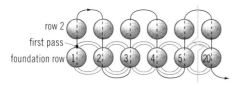

FIGURE 1

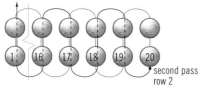

FIGURE 2

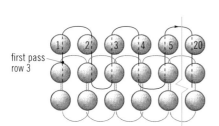

FIGURE 3

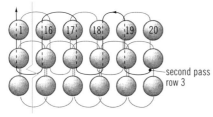

FIGURE 4

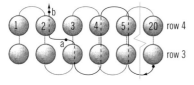

FIGURE 5

degrees so the bead holes are vertical, not horizontal. This will make a graph that is more realistic, with rows that are wider than they are tall.

Basic horizontal square stitch

The foundation row is the widest row, and it's usually in the center of the tile. It has the most threads through it and is thus strong and stable. Use a moderately firm tension; too much tension causes the beadwork to buckle.

[1] Start in the middle of a 3½-yd. (3.2m) length of thread. Form the foundation row with ladder stitch (see Techniques, p. 10), leaving a 2–3 in. (5–7.6cm) tail. Work from left to right, following the chart for pansy #1, above. The outlined foundation row has 20 beads. Exit the top of the left-most bead.

[2] Each row of horizontal square stitch consists of two passes: Work the first from left to right, adding two beads at a time (**figure 1**). Pick up the first two beads of row 2 (the row above the foundation row) and go down the second bead of the foundation row. Come up the third

bead of the foundation row, *pick up the next two beads of row 2 and go down the next bead of the foundation row (the fourth). Come up the next foundation bead (the fifth) and repeat from * until you've added beads 19 and 20 and gone down the twentieth bead of the foundation row. Notice that the beads are in groups of two across the row (**photo a**).

[3] Complete row 2 with the second pass from right to left, which ties the beads of the new row together: With the needle exiting the bottom of the last bead in the foundation row, go up the next-to-last bead (19) and through the 19th and 18th beads of row 2. Go down the next bead of the foundation row (18) and come up the next bead (17). Repeat across until you exit the top of the first bead of row 2 (**figure 2**).

[4] Work rows 3 and 4 like row 2, except don't go through the foundation row again. You only work on two rows at a time, the one you're building and the one below (**figures 3** and **4** and **photo b**).

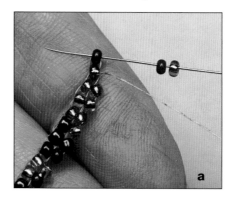

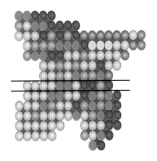

PANSY 3

Decreasing

[1] Continue following the chart, noticing that rows 5, 7, 8, and 9 all begin with a one-bead decrease. Start a row one bead to the right of the edge as follows:

When making the second pass on the new row (row 4), come up through the lower bead of the third stack of beads from the left (**figure 5, point a**). Continue through the second bead on the new row (**a–b**). This positions you to start the decrease row.

[2] Begin the new row, which has an odd number of beads, as usual (**figure 6**). When you have added the next-to-last bead at the end of row 5, your needle will be exiting the bottom of the nineteenth bead on row 4. Come up the last bead of row 4 (#20) and pick up the last bead of row 5 (#19) (**figure 7**). Continue down the two beads to its left and complete the second pass.

[3] To decrease at the end of a row with an even number of beads (i.e. row 6), just stop adding pairs of beads where the new row ends and complete the second pass as usual.

[4] To decrease at the end of a row with an odd number of beads (i.e. row 9), add the next-to-last bead of the new row, and come up the next-to-last bead on the row below (**figure 8, a–c**). Pick up the last bead of the new row, and go down the two beads to its left (**b–c**). Complete the second pass as usual.

[5] When a row begins with a large decrease (i.e. row 10, which decreases by three beads), weave back through the beadwork until you reach the

proper place to begin the row. Notice that in row 10, which decreases an odd number of beads at the beginning, you can weave back only two columns (**figure 9, a–b**). Then you must jog to the right between columns 3 and 4 on row 9 so you're positioned to begin row 10 (**b–c**).

[6] When you have finished the top row, secure the tail with a few half-hitch knots (Techniques) between beads, and trim. Turn the work over, and complete the other half of the flower with the tail.

Increasing

If your design requires you to increase, as do pansies #2 and #3, do so at the end of a thread pass.

[1] If the increase is at the end of a row, add the beads for the new row as usual until you reach the right-hand edge of the existing beadwork. Add the number of beads required at the right edge of the new row one-by-one with ladder stitch (**figure 10, a–b**).

[2] Work back through the ladder (**b–c**), and complete the second pass as usual (**c–d**).

[3] To increase on the left-hand edge of a piece, work the new row from left to right without the decrease. Complete the second pass and then make the increase stitches using ladder stitch. Work an odd number of increase stitches as shown in **figure 10** (**d–e**).

[4] If the ladder increase is an even number of beads, work as shown in **figure 11**.

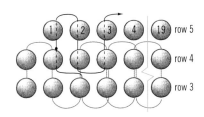

FIGURE 6

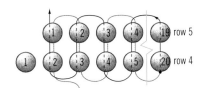

FIGURE 7

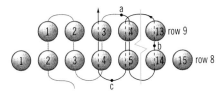

FIGURE 8

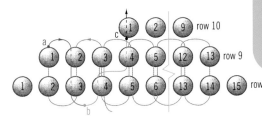

FIGURE 9

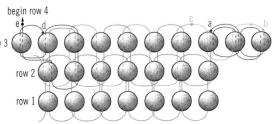

FIGURE 10

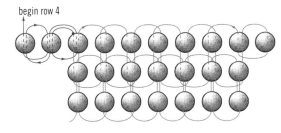

FIGURE 11

PATTERNS

starting knot

FIGURE 12

Finishing

Choose from the following options to make a pin, earrings, or a necklace.

• Sew a pin back to a single pansy about a third of the way from the top. Add fringe from the bottom row.

• Make a pansy earring by opening the loop on an earring wire and hooking it through the top row of beads. Close the loop. If desired, hang accent beads as fringe. Make a second earring to match the first.

• String several pansy tiles together with accent beads and a clasp to create your own necklace:

[**1**] Thread both ends of an 18-in. (46cm) length of bead cord through the eye of a twisted wire needle.

[**2**] Bring the needle from back to front under an edge thread bridge on the center tile where you want the necklace strand to be located. Bring the needle over the thread bridge and through the loop of the doubled cord (**figure 12**). Tighten the knot.

[**3**] String beads as desired, and bring the needle under a thread bridge on the second tile. Tighten.

[**4**] Sew back into the strand, and tie a few half-hitch knots. Dot the knots with G-S Hypo Cement, and trim the tail.

[**5**] Repeat steps 1–4 to join the rest of the tiles and to attach the clasp.

MATERIALS

all projects
• size 11º seed beads in each of **10** colors (for 1 pansy):
  7g **6** shades of purple
  2g **3** shades of green
  1g yellow
• Nymo 0 or 00, conditioned with beeswax
• beading needles, #12 or #13

necklace 20 in. (51cm)
• assorted accent beads
• clasp
• nylon bead-stringing cord, size 1 or 0
• twisted-wire beading needles
• G-S Hypo Cement

earrings
• assorted accent beads (optional)
• pair of earring wires
• chainnose pliers

pin
• assorted accent and seed beads (optional)
• pin back

TEXTURES

Textural options abound with seed beads. From slinky fringe to leafy branches to loops, ruffles, and bubbles, seed beads give you the flexibility to string, stitch, and sculpt your beads into almost anything imaginable. With a few basic techniques, you can create rich surface textures and embellishments. Use seed beads to explore the wide variety of shapes, textures, and objects you can make.

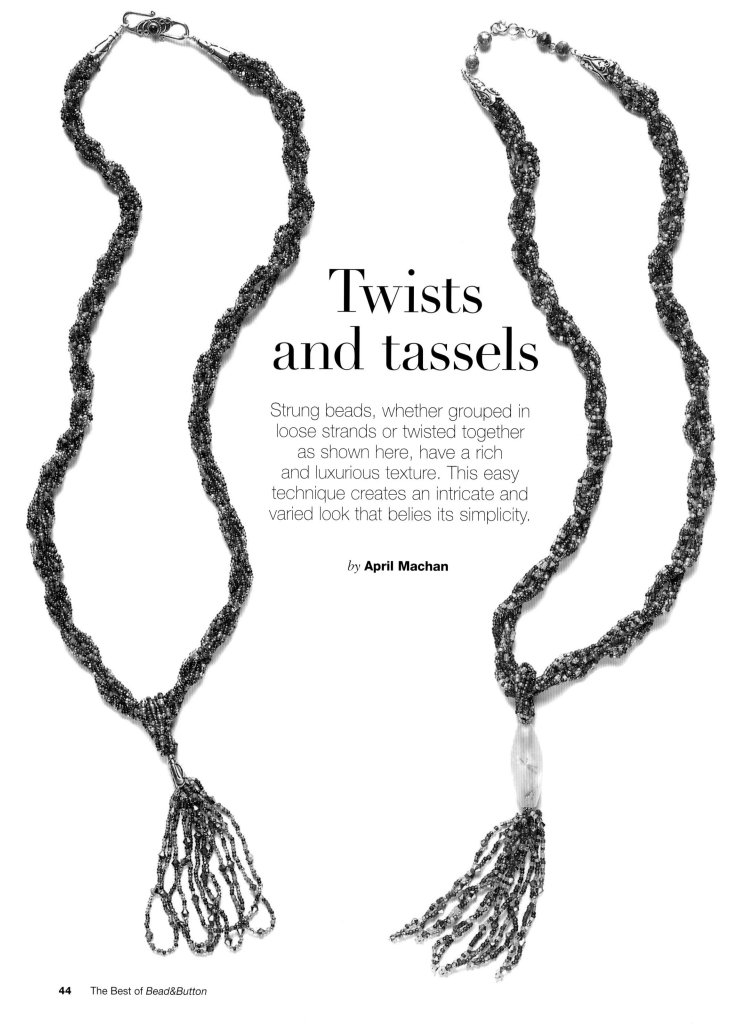

Twists and tassels

Strung beads, whether grouped in loose strands or twisted together as shown here, have a rich and luxurious texture. This easy technique creates an intricate and varied look that belies its simplicity.

by **April Machan**

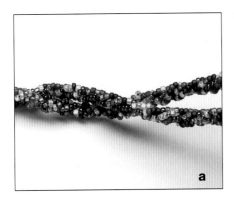

a

b

c

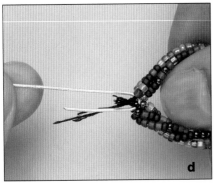

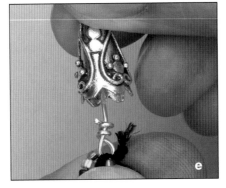

d

e

f

MATERIALS

necklace 16 in. (41cm)

- hank size 11º seed beads
- **3** 18mm cones or **2** cones and **1** artist bead (Alethia Donothan, DAC Beads, dacbeads.com)
- **36** 4mm bicone crystals
- **4** 6mm round crystals or pearls
- 12 in. (30cm) 22-gauge wire
- clasp
- Silamide
- beading needles, #10
- G-S Hypo Cement
- chainnose pliers
- roundnose pliers
- wire cutters

Necklace

[1] Cut four 2-yd. (1.8m) lengths of beading thread. Leaving a 2-in. (5cm) tail, hold the strands together with the ends even, and tie an overhand knot (see Techniques, p. 10). Glue the knot.

[2] Thread a needle on one of the strands. Transfer beads from a hank (see Editor's Note on p. 46) or string them until you are 3 in. (7.6cm) from the end of the thread. Tighten the beads along the strand. Create a stop bead by looping through the last bead again in the same direction.

[3] String the other strands as in step 2. Tie the strand ends together with an overhand knot right against the stop beads. Don't remove the second thread pass from the stop beads.

[4] Tape one end of the group of strands to a tabletop. Twist the other end until the beads begin to kink (**photo a**). Touch the rope at its center point, and it will start to twist back on itself (**photo b**). Bring the tail ends of the rope together and a permanent twist will form. **Photo c** shows the rope twisting back on itself from the center point, which now becomes an end of the beaded rope.

[5] Tie the tails together with a surgeon's knot (Techniques) and glue the knot.

[6] Cut a 2½-in. (6.4cm) piece of 22-gauge wire, and bend it ¾ in. (1.9cm) from one end to form a hook. Slide the hook through the knotted end of the rope (**photo d**). Cross the wires, and wrap the short end around the longer wire. Slide a cone on the wire (**photo e**). Make a right-angle bend above the cone (**photo f**) and make a wrapped loop (Techniques). Repeat at the other end of the necklace, slipping the hook through the fold in the twisted rope.

[7] Cut a 2-in. piece of wire. Make a plain loop at one end (Techniques). Slide a 6mm bead close to the loop, and make another loop perpendicular to the first. Repeat to make another beaded link. Open a loop (Techniques) on one end of a link, and join it to the other link. Close the loop. Attach the end loop of the second link to the wrapped loop above one cone on the twisted rope.

[8] Repeat step 7 at the other end of the necklace.

[9] Open the last loop on the beaded link at one end of the necklace. Slide one clasp half onto the loop, then close the loop (**photo g**). Attach the other clasp half to the opposite end of the rope.

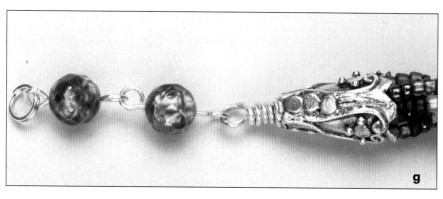

g

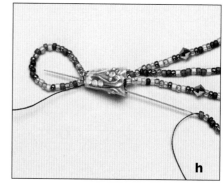

h

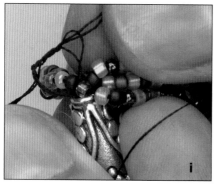

i

Tassel with cone
Blue necklace, right; purple-and-silver necklace, p. 44

[1] Thread a needle with 1½ yd. (1.4m) of Nymo. Leaving a 3-in. (7.6cm) tail, string a cone, narrow end first. Tape the tail to the outside of the cone.
[2] String 6 in. (15cm) of seed beads and crystals, and go back through the cone in the opposite direction.
[3] String 35 seed beads, and go back through the cone, forming a loop.
[4] Repeat steps 2 and 3 (**photo h**) for a total of five loops above and six loops below the cone. End with the needle exiting the top of the cone. Leave a 3-in. tail.
[5] Remove the tape applied in step 1, and tie the tails together with a surgeon's knot (Techniques and **photo i**). Glue the knot. When dry, attach a needle to one tail, and work it through several beads in any loop. Trim the excess thread, and repeat with the other tail.
[6] Slide the loop of the tassel over the twisted rope.

Tassel with artist bead
Blue-and-green necklace, p. 44

Follow steps 1–4 of "Tassel with cone," substituting a focal bead for the cone. To add a twist to the fringe, exit the bottom of the bead, string 6 in. of seed beads and crystals, and twist the thread by rolling the needle between your thumb and forefinger. Check the amount of twist by bringing the end of the strand up to the focal bead. If the beaded strand twists up, it will stay twisted. Go back through the focal bead. Add a twist to all the loops below the focal bead. Follow steps 4–6 of "Tassel with cone" to finish.

STRINGING BEADS FROM THE HANK
1. Carefully cut one end of the strand near the hank's knot.
2. Pull the strand straight and run the needle and thread (or flexible beading wire) into the beads on the strand (**photo**, below).
3. Slide the beads from the hank onto the new stringing material.

Passion flower

Texture and color combine to create a stunning three-dimensional floral centerpiece. Your friends will be amazed to learn you made this with little more than seed beads and craft wire.

by **Dorothy Bonitz**

Refer to the flower illustration on p. 48 as you work.

Petals and leaves

[1] Transfer one strand of color A beads onto the spool of 26-gauge white or gold wire.
[2] Working 3 in. (7.6cm) from the end of the wire, form 3¾ in. (9.5cm) of beads into a loop and twist the wires together a few times to secure them (**photo a**).
[3] Position the working wire lengthwise through the center of the petal and slide enough beads down to fill the space between the base and tip of the petal (**photo b**).
[4] Wrap the wire over the tip

a

b

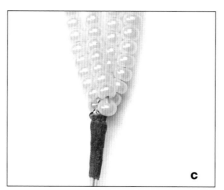

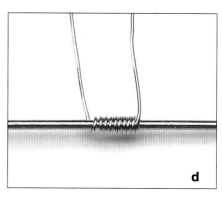

c

d

e

f

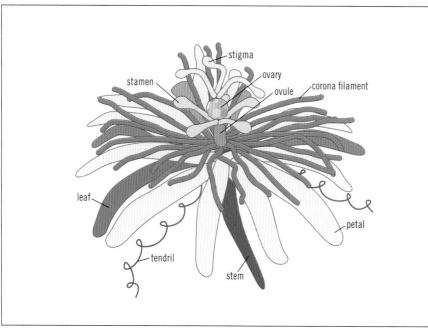

between the end beads, and slide down enough beads to fill the space between the tip and the base. Twist the wires together at the base to secure them.

[5] Cut the working wire from the spool so it is even with the 3-in. tail.

[6] Cut the end of the green floral tape at an angle and in half lengthwise. Place the tapered end at the base of the petal and wrap it around the wires for ¼ in. (6mm) (**photo c**).

[7] Make a total of ten color A, four-row crossover petals.

[8] Make five four-row crossover leaves using 26-gauge green wire and color B seed beads.

Corona filaments

[1] Cut a 10-in. (25cm) piece of 28-gauge gold wire, and fold it in half.

[2] Place the corsage pin in the fold, and wrap one end of the wire around the pin eight to ten times (**photo d**).

[3] Remove the coil from the pin, and cut it in half through the coil.

[4] On one wire, string 1 in. (2.5cm) of color C beads, one color D bead, two color E beads, one D, and ½ in. (1.3cm) of Cs (**photo e**).

[5] Repeat step 4 with the remaining wire. Then twist the straight ends of the wires together just below the beads.

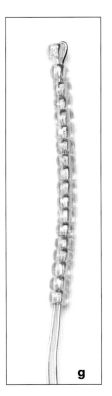

g

h

i

[6] Make a total of 35 corona filaments (17 pairs and one single).
[7] Cut a piece of floral tape as you did for the petals. Tape together two pairs by wrapping the tape around the wires just under the beads for ¼ in.
[8] Repeat step 7 with the remaining wires. You will have eight groups of four and one of three.

Stamens
[1] Cut an 8-in. (20cm) piece of 28-gauge gold wire.
[2] String seven color F beads to the center of the wire. Form them into a loop by twisting the wires together beneath the beads.
[3] Position the wire ends side by side and string six Fs over both wires (**photo f**). Secure the beads in place with a ¼-in. wrap of floral tape.
[4] Make a total of five stamens.

Stigmas
[1] Transfer the color E beads onto the spool of 28-gauge gold wire.
[2] Slide the beads 3 in. from the end of the wire, skip the end bead, and bring the wire back through 1 in. of beads (**photo g**). Push the beads up against the end bead and cut the spool wire flush with the short wire.
[3] Make a total of three stigmas.

Tendrils
[1] Cut three pieces of 28-gauge gold wire to the following lengths: 7 in. (18cm), 9 in. (23cm), and 11 in. (28cm).
[2] Wrap each wire with brown floral tape. Coil the wires around a skewer.
[3] Shape the wires as desired (**photo h**).

Assembly
[1] Hold the three stigmas together, and slide the 8mm bead over all three wires and against the seed beads.
[2] Arrange the five stamen parts below the 8mm bead. Wrap the wires together with 28-gauge gold wire.
[3] Starting just below the stamens, wrap about 1 in. of the wires with green floral tape to hold the parts in place.
[4] Arrange the corona filaments ½ in. below the stamen so some tape shows on the stem (**photo i**). Wire a couple groups to the stem at a time, then secure with floral tape as before. Wrap the stem with floral tape several times at this point to give it a wider base.
[5] Arrange the flower petals, leaves, and tendrils next. At this point you can start to cut some of the stem wires to form the stalk into the desired shape.
[6] Wrap the entire stem with floral tape.
[7] Shape the flower as shown in the illustration.

MATERIALS
one flower
- 8mm glass bead, pale green or white
- size 11º seed beads
  12g pearl white, color A
  10g medium to dark green, color B
  5g purple, color C
  5g dark purple, color D
  2g white in crystal or transparent white-lined, color E
  3g lime green, color F
- 26-gauge craft wire, green and white or gold
- 28-gauge craft wire, gold
- corsage pin
- floral tape, brown and green
- wood barbecue skewer or mandrel with 2–3mm diameter
- chainnose pliers
- wire cutters

Fringed collar

A variety of seed-bead types contributes to the slinky smooth texture of this fringed necklace. Remember that your selection of bead sizes will affect the length of each strand, so plan carefully before you begin.

by **Kathy Rice**

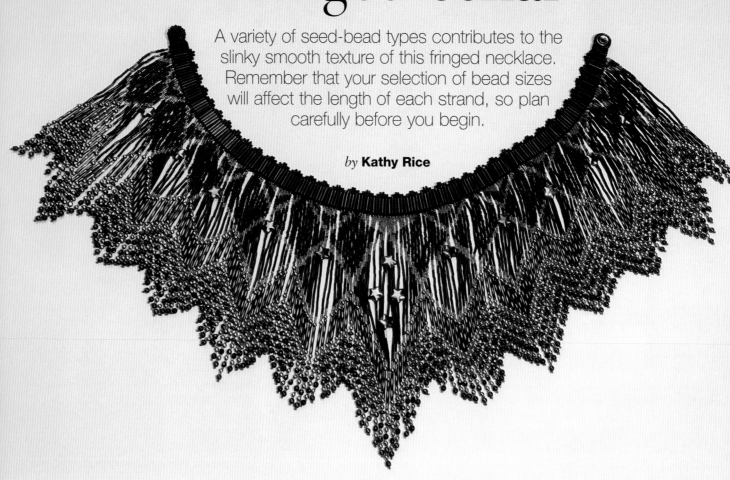

Beaded clasp

[1] Sew each snap half to a small piece of leather or Ultrasuede, and trim the fabric to about one bead's width larger than the snap.

[2] Thread a needle with a 1-yd. (.9m) length of conditioned Nymo (see Techniques, p. 10), and make an overhand knot (Techniques) at the end. On one snap half, insert the needle into the leather from the top. (The snap fastener is on the bottom.) Pick up two 11º seed beads, and sew back through the leather, working close to the snap (figure 1, a–b). Pick up two seed beads, go through the first hole, and go back to the bottom (b–c). Go through the first two seed beads again (c–d).

[3] Continue adding two beads at a time on each side until you've gone completely around the edge of the snap. Don't crowd the beads.

Reinforce the beads on the bottom by running the needle through each bead in the circle again (figure 2).

[4] Bring the needle through the leather to the top, and take it through one of the beads in the circle. Fill the inside of the circle as follows: Pick up a bead, skip a bead, and go through the next bead in the circle (figure 3, a–b). Repeat this as you work around the inside of the circle (b–c). Make sure the beads lie flat without any large gaps. Pass the needle through all the beads in this new circle again (c–d).

[5] Depending on the snap size, you may need to weave another circle. Otherwise, just fill in any gaps.

[6] Work in square stitch (Techniques) to attach approximately four to eight 11º seed beads to the beads along one edge of the snap (figure 4). This row of seed beads should equal the length of the bugle bead you plan to use for the collar base. Keep the beads in as straight a line as possible.

[7] Make two rows of two-bead square stitch, adding the same number of beads as in step 6 (figure 5).

[8] Repeat steps 2–7 for the other snap component.

Collar base

This collar base consists of 192 12mm bugle beads interspersed with 11ºs. If you alter the length, be sure the number of bugles is divisible by six.

[1] Attach a 12mm bugle bead to the last row of square stitch on one snap component by sewing through the seed beads and the bugle bead several times (figure 6, a–b).

[2] Working in ladder stitch (Techniques), add five bugle beads and one seed bead (b–c).

[3] Repeat step 2 36 times. Finish by adding six bugle beads to the collar base, and attaching the other snap fastener to the last bugle bead as before.

[4] Attach a seed bead to the bottom edge of each bugle bead using brick stitch (Techniques). Pass the thread through the spacer beads when you reach them (**figure 7**).

[5] To make the picot edging, secure a new thread and go up through the first bugle bead on one end of the collar. Pick up three seed beads, sew under the thread bridge between the first and second bugle beads, and go back up the last seed bead, (**figure 8, a–b**). Pick up two seed beads, go under the next thread bridge, and go back through the last seed bead (**b–c**). Repeat across the top of the collar base. Zigzag back through several rows of beads, tie a few half-hitch knots (Techniques), and trim.

Beaded fringe

[1] Use graph paper and colored pencils to design a fringe for your necklace, allowing one strand of fringe for every bugle bead on your collar base. Make the graph the actual length of the fringe. It's important to include long strands of fringe at the back of the necklace to balance the weight at the front. The fringe in this necklace ranges from 4½–7½ in. (11.4–19.1cm).

[2] Calculate the quantities of beads to complete your design and collect all your materials before you begin.

[3] Thread a needle with 2–3 yds. (1.8–2.7m) of Nymo and secure it in the beadwork. Exit an end bugle, and continue through the seed bead below it. String the beads following your graph. At the bottom of the strand, skip the last bead, and go back through the other fringe beads, being careful not to skip any. Continue up through the seed bead at the collar base and the bugle bead above it. Keep the tension firm, but allow enough slack in the strands to give the fringe movement.

[4] Go down through the next bugle and seed bead and continue adding fringe to the collar base. Secure the tail in the beadwork and trim.

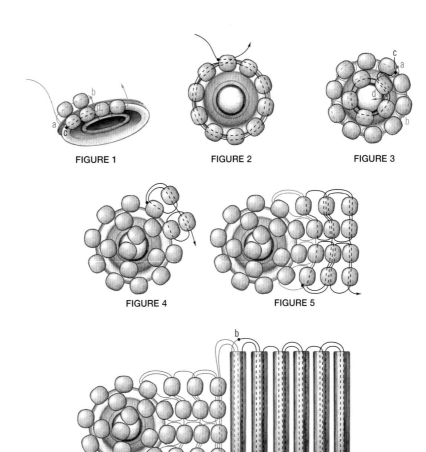

FIGURE 1

FIGURE 2

FIGURE 3

FIGURE 4

FIGURE 5

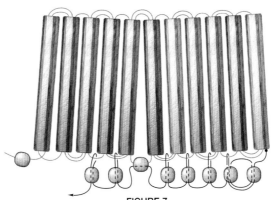

FIGURE 6

FIGURE 7

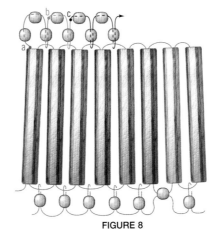

FIGURE 8

MATERIALS
necklace 16 in. (41cm)

- 30g 12mm bugle beads
- 40g size 11º seed, bugle, and accent beads in assorted colors for fringe
- heavy-duty snap
- Nymo D, conditioned with beeswax
- beading needles, #10 or #12
- small piece of leather or Ultrasuede
- package ½ in. (1.3cm) black seam binding
- graph paper
- colored pencils

TEXTURES

Leafy fringe necklace

Make a simple necklace more complex by embellishing it with branched fringe and multicolored glass leaf beads.

by **Lea Nowicki**

Necklace base

[1] Center 36 8° seed beads on 2 ft. (61cm) of flexible beading wire. Tape one end.

[2] String a leaf, pointed end first, then six 8°s (**photo a**).

[3] String a leaf, round end first, an 8°, a leaf, pointed end first, and six 8°s (**photo b**).

[4] Repeat step 3 twice, alternating the leaf colors (**photo c**).

[5] String a crimp bead and the clasp, then go back through the crimp and the next few 8°s.

[6] Repeat steps 2–5 on the other end of the necklace.

[7] Check the fit, and add or remove beads if necessary. Crimp the crimp bead (see Techniques, p. 10 and **photo d**), and then trim the excess wire.

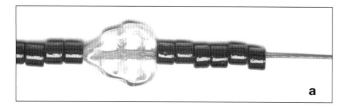

a

b

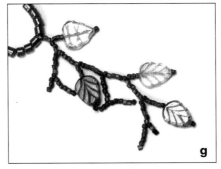

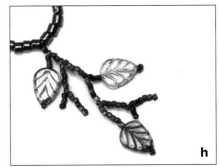

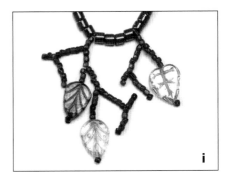

Fringed center

[1] Thread a needle with 1 yd. (.9m) of Fireline. Tie the line to the base necklace with a half-hitch knot (Techniques), placing the knot two beads from the center. Go through two beads toward the center and make another knot.

[2] Refer to the fringe illustration below. Pick up 36 Charlottes, a leaf, and another Charlotte. Turn, skip the last bead, and go back through the leaf and six beads (**figure, a–b**).

[3] Pick up 12 Charlottes. Turn, skip the last bead, and go back through the next five beads (**b–c**).

[4] Pick up three Charlottes. Turn, skip the last bead, and go back through the next two beads. Continue through the next six beads toward the stem, then go up through six more beads (**c–d** and **photo e**).

[5] Pick up three Charlottes, a leaf, and a Charlotte. Turn, skip the last bead, and go back through the leaf and three beads. Go up through the next six beads (**d–e** and **photo f**).

[6] Repeat steps 3–5 twice. Go through the last three Charlottes to finish the fringe (**e–f** and **photo g**).

[7] Go through four 8°s, then make a half-hitch knot. Pick up 24 Charlottes and make the next fringe with three leaves (**photo h**).

[8] Repeat step 7 twice, picking up 18 Charlottes and making the fringe with two leaves (**photo i, left**).

[9] Repeat step 7 once, picking up nine Charlottes and making the fringe with one leaf (**photo i, right**).

[10] When you've made the last fringe on the end, tie a half-hitch knot, go through an 8°, then tie another knot. Sew through a few more beads. Dot the knots with glue, let dry, and trim the Fireline.

[11] Repeat steps 1–10 to add fringe to the other side.

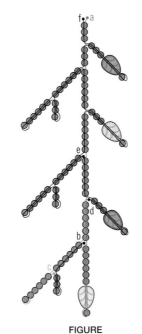

FIGURE

MATERIALS

necklace 16 in. (41cm)

- **34** pressed glass leaves in four colors
- 10g size 8° seed beads
- 5g size 13° Charlottes or cut seed beads
- 2 yd. (1.8cm) Fireline, 6-lb. test
- 2 ft. (60cm) flexible beading wire, .014
- toggle clasp
- **2** crimp beads
- beading needles, #12
- crimping pliers
- wire cutters

EDITOR'S NOTE:

Making fringe is the most time-consuming part of this project, so change the bead count, increase the bead size, or simplify the design to fit your needs.

TEXTURES

Hoop earrings

A beaded hoop earring technique offers many variations. Create a variety of fun textures from retro loops to spiky branched fringe.

by **Ella Johnson-Bentley**

Foundation row

[1] Thread a needle with 2 yd. (1.8m) of conditioned Nymo (see Techniques, p. 10). Use a square knot (Techniques) to tie it to the top left-hand side of the hoop. Pick up one color A seed bead, and slide it down to the hoop. Holding the tail alongside the hoop, bring the needle to the inside of the hoop from the back and then through the bead you just added, encircling the hoop and tail (**photo a**).

[2] Pick up a bead, slide it down to the hoop, hold it in place and proceed as with the first bead. Hold the tail until you've added nine beads, then cut it. Continue adding single beads all the

way around the hoop. Then finish with one of the following earring variations.

Jack Frost fringe

[1] After finishing the foundation row, weave your thread back through six or seven beads. The needle must exit pointing away from the hoop.

[2] Pick up six color A beads and one color B bead. Skip the B, and go back through the last two As. Pick up four As and a B. Go back through the four As and two As on the stem (**photo b**). Pick up four As and a B. Go back through the As, the last two stem beads, and the foundation bead.

[3] Go through the next foundation bead, and repeat step 2. Continue making branches off every foundation bead until you are six or seven beads from the end.

[4] Weave through three beads on the foundation row, and tie a half-hitch knot (Techniques) between two beads on the hoop. Repeat. Glue each knot with G-S Hypo Cement for security.

[5] String the accent beads on a head pin. Make a plain loop (Techniques) against the top bead. Open the loop (Techniques) above the beads, attach the dangle to the hoop, and close the

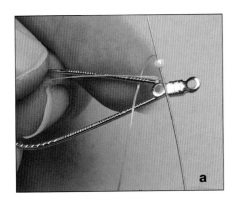
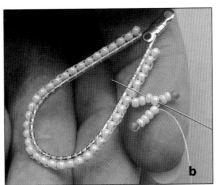
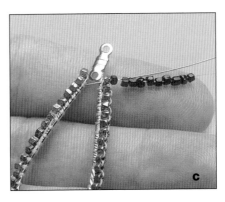

loop. Open the earring wire's loop, attach the hoop, then close the loop.
[6] Make a second earring to match the first.

Sunburst fringe

[1] After the foundation row, weave the thread through the last two beads added. Then weave back out the end bead to secure the base and be positioned for the fringe.

[2] Pick up ten size 12º beads. Go back through the first bead added and the first foundation row bead (**photo c**).

[3] Come out the next foundation bead, and repeat step 2 but string two more beads for a total of 12. Continue around to the center of the hoop, adding two additional beads in each loop. At the center, decrease by taking away two beads per loop to the end.

[4] Sew through two foundation row beads. Make a half-hitch knot (Techniques), and sew through two more beads. Knot again, and go through a few additional beads before trimming the thread. Seal the knots with G-S Hypo Cement.

[5] Add a dangle as in step 5 of the Jack Frost earrings.

[6] Make a second earring to match the first.

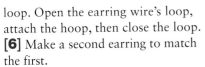

MATERIALS
both projects
- **2** beading hoops with loops (firemountaingems.com)
- **2** 2-in. (5cm) headpins
- accent beads for center dangle
- beading needle, #13
- Nymo O, conditioned with beeswax
- pair of earring wires
- chainnose pliers
- roundnose pliers
- wire cutter
- G-S Hypo Cement

Jack Frost earrings
- size 11º seed beads
  5g color A
  2g color B

Sunburst earrings
- **70-80** size 10º 3-cut seed beads, color A
- hank size 12º 3-cut seed beads, color B

MAKE YOUR OWN HOOP FINDINGS

1. Cut an 8-in. (20cm) piece of 20-gauge wire. Make a plain loop (Techniques) at one end. Make a wrapped loop (Techniques) 3/16 in. (5mm) from the plain loop, and continue wrapping until you reach the plain loop (**top photo**).

2. Gently shape the wire into a teardrop hoop, bringing the tail up to meet the wraps near the plain loop.

3. Wrap over the wraps between loops (**bottom photo**). Trim the excess wire.

TEXTURES

Garden necklace

Small beaded flowers and leaves accentuate a floral bead centerpiece. The sculptural nature of the flowers creates a natural complement to the art bead.

by **Misty Leppard**

MATERIALS
necklace 18 in. (46cm)

- 20–30mm art bead
- **2** 8mm rondelles with small holes
- 3–5g size 11º seed beads in each of **11** colors
  light purple, color A
  dark purple, color B
  hot pink, color C
  red, color D
  dark blue, color E
  light blue, color F
  lilac, color G
  gold, color H
  yellow, color I
  dark green, color J
  light green, color K
- 2g size 8º seed beads
- **2** size 6º seed beads
- hank size 13º Charlottes, white
- flexible beading wire, green
- Nymo 0, conditioned with beeswax or Thread Heaven
- 2 in. (5cm) gold wire, 18-gauge
- **2** crimp beads
- beading needles, #12
- clasp
- G-S Hypo Cement
- chainnose pliers
- crimping pliers
- roundnose pliers
- wire cutters
- clothes pin or hemostat

Make all the buds and flowers with a modified tubular-peyote stitch (see Techniques, p. 10) before starting the necklace construction. Try the buds first. They don't require any increasing or decreasing, but they do require tight tension.

It's easier to identify each row if you use more than one bead color in a bud or flower. All the flowers are made without the center bead. You'll add it when you string the flower on a vine.

Making the flowers

[1] Thread a needle with a 1-yd. (.9m) length of waxed thread (Techniques). String the first three beads of the bud or flower, leaving a 4-in. (10cm) tail.
[2] Tie the beads into a circle and, working in peyote stitch, follow one of the charts and directions on pages 57 and 58 to make a bud or flower. When the bud is complete, weave in the thread, skip 9 in. (23cm) of thread, and begin the next bud on the same thread.
[3] When you've completed all your buds and flowers, cut them apart, secure the tails with half-hitch knots (Techniques), and trim the tails.

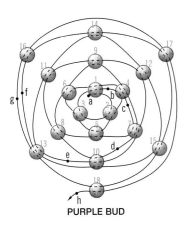

PURPLE BUD

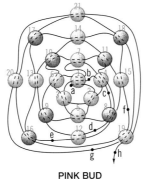

PINK BUD

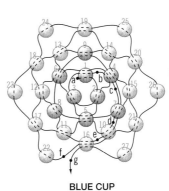

BLUE CUP

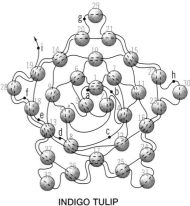

INDIGO TULIP

Purple bud

Row 1: Pick up three color A beads (**a–b**).
Row 2: Pick up three Bs (**b–c**).
Row 3: Three As (**c–d**).
Row 4: Three Bs (**d–e**).
Row 5: Three As (**e–f**).
Row 6: Three Bs (**f–g**).

Go through the beads in row 6 again and pull snug. Sew through a few beads, tie a half-hitch knot, repeat, and trim. Seal the knots with G-S Hypo Cement. Weave in the tail, and trim.

Pink bud

Row 1: Three color C beads (**a–b**).
Row 2: Four Cs. Place the increase between bead 1 and bead 4, as shown on the chart (**b–c**).
Row 3: Four Ds (**c–d**).
Row 4: Four Cs (**d–e**).
Row 5: Three Ds (**e–f**).
Row 6: Three Cs (**f–g**).

Go through last the last three beads again (**g–h**). Go through a few beads, secure the thread, and trim, as in the purple bud.

Blue cup

Row 1: Three color E beads (**a–b**).
Row 2: Three Es (**b–c**).
Row 3: Three Es (**c–d**).
Row 4: Six Fs (**d–e**).
Row 5: Six Fs (**e–f**).
Optional Row 6: Six Fs (**f–g**).
Secure the tails, and trim.

Indigo tulip

Row 1: Three color B beads (**a–b**).
Row 2: Four Bs, adding bead 7 between beads 1 and 4 (**b–c**).
Row 3: Five Gs, adding bead 12 between beads 4 and 8 (**c–d**).
Row 4: Five Bs, adding bead 17 between beads 12 and 8 (**d–e**).
Row 5: Ten Gs, adding two Gs between each B.
Row 6: Five Gs. Step up through the first G added in this round (**e–f**).
Secure the tails, and trim.

Seed Bead Savvy **57**

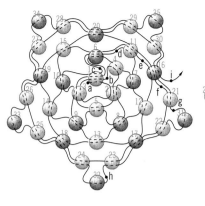

RED TULIP

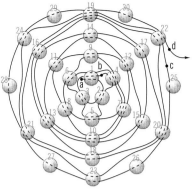

DAFFODIL CENTER

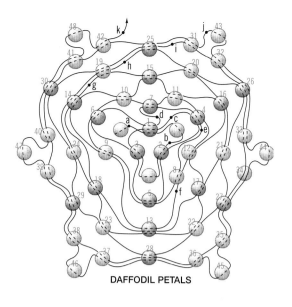

DAFFODIL PETALS

Red tulip
Row 1: Three color C beads (**a–b**).
Row 2: Two Cs (**b–c**).
Row 3: Five Ds (**c–d**).
Row 4: Five Cs (**d–e**).
Row 5: Five Ds (**e–f**).
Row 6: Ten Cs, adding two Cs between the Ds. Step up through only the first bead of the first pair added in this step (**f–g**).
Row 7: Five Ds. Add bead 31, go through three beads (**g–h**), add bead 32, go through three beads (**h–i**), and continue around (**i–j**).
    Secure the tails, and trim.

Daffodil
Because the Charlottes are so small, do not tie knots until the end. Start with about 1 yd. (.9m) of thread.

White center
Row 1: Three Charlottes (**a–b**).
Rows 2–8: Add three Charlottes per row (**b–c**).
Row 9: Six Charlottes, adding one bead between each bead in rows 7 and 8 (**c–d**). Weave through to the first row, and set aside.
    Secure the tail, avoiding the first row, and trim.

Daffodil petals
Row 1: With the original needle, pick up one color H bead, and go through a bead in the first row of the white center. Repeat, adding two more Hs (**b–c**).
Row 2: Three Hs (**c–d**). Add a fourth H to row 2 between beads 1 and 4 (**d–e**).
Row 3: Five Is. Bead 12 goes between beads 4 and 8 (**e–f**).
Row 4: Six Hs. The last one goes between beads 13 and 14 (**f–g**).
Row 5: Six Is (**g–h**).
Row 6: Six Hs (**h–i**).
Row 7: Two Is between the Hs, 12 Is total. Step up through only the first I added on this round (**i–j**).
Row 8: One I between each pair of Is in row 7 (**j–k**).
    Secure the tails, and trim.

Leaves
Make the leaves as you string the vines.
    Pick up six or seven color J or K beads, skip a bead, and go through the next bead to make a point (**a–b**).
    Pick up enough Js or Ks to reach the bottom of the leaf, and come up through the bottom of bead 2 (**b–c**).
    Pick up enough beads to fill the center, and go up the bottom bead to one side of the point, and through the bead on the other side of the point (**c–d**). Go through the middle bead(s) (**d–e**) and down through the last bead on the second side and the first bead picked up to begin the leaf (**e–f**). Continue into the vine.

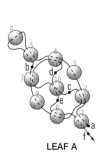

LEAF A

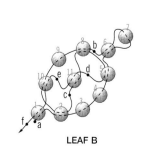

LEAF B

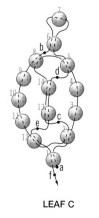

LEAF C

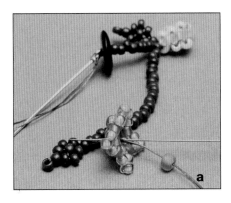

Tassel

Vary the lengths, patterns, and colors of the fringe.

[1] Make a small wrapped loop (Techniques) on one end of the 2-in. (5cm) piece of wire. Thread 4 ft. (1.2m) of green Nymo onto a needle, and double it. Tie the ends of the thread onto the wrapped loop, and dab with glue.

[2] String a rondelle and eight color J or K seed beads, and make a leaf as explained on p. 58. String a bud by going through two beads on the bottom row of the bud and then back through the last bead on the vine.

[3] String 1¼ in. (3.2cm) of green beads, make a leaf, go through the center of a flower from the outside bottom, string an 8º seed bead, and go back through the center of the flower toward the vine (photo a).

[4] Skip a bead on the vine and go through all the vine beads, the rondelle, and the loop on the wire. Go back through the rondelle, and start another fringe. Make the desired number of fringe strands, secure the thread, and trim.

Necklace construction

Decide which color flowers go on which color vine. Here, yellow and blue

> **EDITOR'S NOTE: When stringing a bud or flower, always span its base with two or three beads on the wire before threading the wire through the next length of beads. Pull the wire tight before and after adding leaves, buds, and flowers.**

flowers are paired on the dark-green vine, and pink and purple flowers are paired on the light-green vine.

[1] Compare the length of the tassel's wire and the length of the centerpiece bead. Make a small wrapped loop at the edge of the wire about two-thirds of the bead's length from the tassel. This loop needs to fit inside the bead.

[2] Center the wrapped loop on two 1-yd. lengths of flexible beading wire.

[3] Tie four 5-ft. (1.5m) lengths of thread with needles onto the wire loop. Secure and trim. String the center bead and the second rondelle onto all the strands (photo b). Divide the strands into two equal groups.

[4] Working on one side with one strand of thread, string ¼ in. (6mm) of Js. Put a strand of beading wire through these beads. Make a leaf, and go through two beads on the bottom row of a bud. String ¾ in. (1.9cm) of Js. String two Ks onto the beading wire and run the flexible beading wire through the beads after the bud (photo c).

[5] Make a leaf. String ½ in. (1.3cm) of Js, thread the wire, make a leaf, and string a bud. String ½ in. of beads, thread the wire through the ½ in. of beads, and make a leaf. String ¾ in. beads, thread the wire, and make a leaf. To add a daffodil, go through two beads on the bottom row of the flower. String three Js onto the flexible beading wire. Then take the flexible beading wire through the vine that exits the daffodil. Continue for about 3 in. (7.6cm), then set the vine aside with a clothes pin or hemostat holding it in place.

[6] String ½ in. of Ks onto the second thread on the same side, thread the other length of wire, make a leaf, string ¾ in. of Ks, thread the wire, and make a leaf. Go through the bottom

of a pink flower from the outside, and string an 8º. Go back through the center. String two or three Ks onto the wire. Then string the wire through the vine that exits the flower.

String ½ in. of Ks and the wire, make a leaf, string ¾ in. of Ks and the wire, make a leaf, and add a purple bud. String ¼ in. of Ks and the wire, and make a leaf. Try to make the two lengths of vines even by stringing Js and/or Ks.

[7] Crossing vines: Take both needles and one strand of beading wire through the same single J or K. String a K on the other wire strand.

Continue as before varying the buds, flowers, and leaves.

[8] After about 8 in. (20cm) on one side, secure the vines, and start to work on side two. If side one started with a bud, side two should start with a flower of a contrasting color.

[9] To end the necklace, secure the thread on all four vines after the last leaf or bud by weaving in the tails and tying a few half-hitch knots (Techniques). Add enough Js and Ks to the wires to make the vines the desired length. Put both wire ends from one side of the necklace through a 6º and a crimp bead. String one clasp half and go back through the crimp bead and the 6º. Crimp the crimp bead (Techniques). Trim the wire, and repeat on the other side.

TEXTURES

Sculptural cuff

Embellish a peyote band with a garden of herringbone flowers. This floral texture makes a unique cuff.

by **Bonnie O'Donnell-Painter**

Prepare the base

To determine the length of the peyote band, subtract the length of your clasp from the desired length of the bracelet. The fit needs to be comfortable around your wrist, but not floppy.

[1] Pick up eight, ten, or twelve cylinder beads on a comfortable length of conditioned Nymo (see Techniques, p. 10). Work in even-count peyote (Techniques) until you reach the desired length.

[2] Attach one clasp half to each end of the band. To attach a single- or multistrand clasp, make small bead loops through the clasp loops (**photo a**). Reinforce the loops by going through

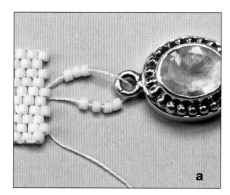

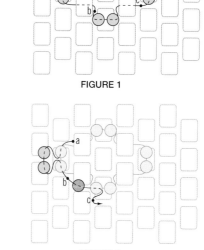

FIGURE 1

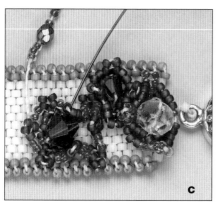

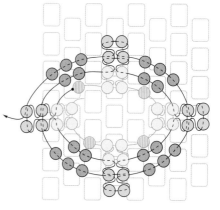

FIGURE 2

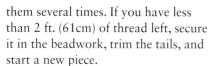

FIGURE 3

them several times. If you have less than 2 ft. (61cm) of thread left, secure it in the beadwork, trim the tails, and start a new piece.

[3] Weave through the base, and exit one of the edge beads at either end. Pick up three color A 15º seed beads, and go under the thread bridge between the first and second edge beads (**photo b**). Pick up three As, and go under the thread bridge between the second and third beads. Repeat, covering both long edges with bead ruffles.

Embellishment

[1] To make the smallest flower, weave through the base, and exit any bead except an edge bead. You can start at the center of the band or at either end. Pick up two 15ºs, and go through a neighboring bead in the same row (**figure 1, a–b**).

[2] Pick up two Bs, skip a row, and go through the next bead (**b–c**).

[3] Pick up two Bs and go through the neighboring bead, as in step 1 (**c–d**).

[4] Pick up two Bs and complete the circle by going through the bead at the starting point (**d–e**).

MATERIALS

bracelet 7 in. (18cm)
- 10g Japanese cylinder beads
- 6g size 15º seed beads, color A
- 3g seed beads, size 15º, each of **3 or more** accent colors, B–D
- assorted crystals, pearls, gemstones, and seed beads
- clasp or button
- Nymo D, conditioned with beeswax or Thread Heaven
- beading needles, #12

[5] Go through the first Bº added in step 1. Pick up two Bs, and go through the next B (**figure 2, a–b**).

[6] Pick up one color C bead, and go through the next B (**b–c**). Continue around the row, adding two spine beads and one accent bead until you reach the starting point.

[7] Work three or four rows, adding one more accent bead between spine beads with each new row (**figure 3**). When you finish a flower, work back through the 15ºs to the peyote base. String an accent bead, and secure it in the flower's center. Then weave through the base beads, and exit where you want to place the next flower.

[8] To make larger flowers, increase the number of spines, as shown in **figure 4**.

[9] Once you've stitched flowers across the band, string 15ºs, crystals, pearls, and other small accent beads and stitch them into place around the flowers (**photo c**). The embellishment can be as dense as you like. Check the reverse side of the base from time to time to make sure no thread shows on the back.

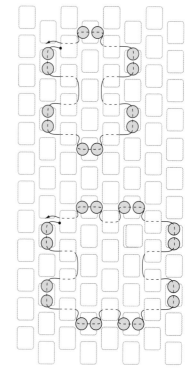

FIGURE 4

Basketweave bracelet

Weave square stitch strips to create a stylish cuff bracelet. The basketweave texture is enhanced by the direction of the beads and the alternating colors.

by **Karen Frankfeldt**

This cuff bracelet should fit comfortably around the wrist without sagging.

Right-angle weave base

[1] Thread a needle with 2 yd. (1.8m) of conditioned Nymo (see Techniques, p. 10). Leave a 6-in. (15cm) tail, and pick up 16 color A seed beads. Tie them in a taut circle using a surgeon's knot (Techniques). Sew through the first eight beads again (**figure 1, a–b**).

[2] Pick up 12 As, and go through the last four As sewn through and the first eight As added in this step (**b–c**).

[3] Repeat step 2 twice, to make a total of four squares (**c–d**).

[4] Pick up 12 As and go through the last four As sewn through and the 12 As just added (**d–e**).

[5] To begin the next row, pick up 12 As and go through the last four As sewn through and the first four As added (**figure 2, a–b**).

[6] Pick up eight beads and go through the bottom four As of the second square in the previous row, four As on the side of the square just completed, and the eight As added

(**b–c**). Sew through the bottom four As on the next square (**c–d**).

[7] Continue in right-angle weave (RAW) to make two more squares, and go through the last four beads on the bottom of the previous row (**d–e**).

[8] Pick up eight As. Sew through the side of the last square stitched and the bottom of the first square again. Go through all eight As (**e–f**).

[9] Repeat steps 5–8 until the bracelet is long enough to fit around your wrist with at least a ½-in. (1.3cm) gap for the closure. This bracelet's base is 22 squares long.

Closure

[1] Sew through the beadwork to exit the end bead of one long side.

[2] Continue through the four As on the square's outer edge, pick up an A, and sew through the four edge beads on the next square. Repeat across the row to fill the gaps.

[3] Work seven rows of two-bead square stitch (Techniques) to complete this end of the band. Sew a button securely at the center of this panel. Sew into the beadwork, secure the tail with

a few half-hitch knots (Techniques), and trim.

[4] On the opposite end of the base, repeat steps 1–3, completing one row of two-bead square stitch. Turn the work, and weave over to the sixth bead to begin the second row of square stitch (**figure 3, point a**). End this row at **point b**. Turn the piece, and do another row the same length.

[5] Turn the work, and weave through to the fourth bead to begin the third row (**figure 3, point c**). End at **point d**. Turn, and do another row the same length.

[6] To make the loop closure, go through all the beads on the last square stitch row (**e–f**). String enough beads to make a loop that will fit over the button (**f–g**). Go through the entire row of square stitch. Check that the loop fits over the button. Repeat the thread path two or three times. Secure the tail, and trim.

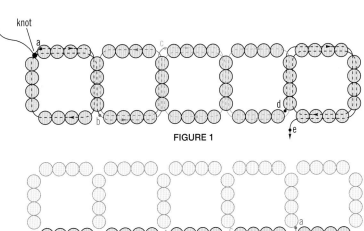

FIGURE 1

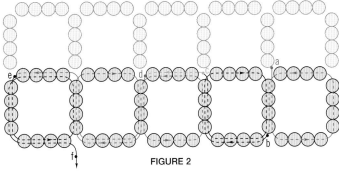

FIGURE 2

MATERIALS

bracelet 6½ in. (16.5cm)

- 20g size 11º Japanese seed beads, in each of **3** colors, A, B, and C
- bead or button for clasp
- beading needles, #12
- Nymo D, conditioned with beeswax

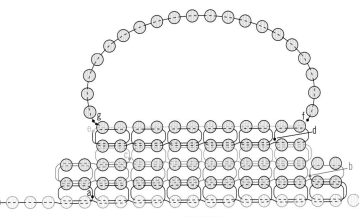

FIGURE 3

Woven strips

[1] Exiting the first bead of the top edge of the RAW square next to a closure strip, pick up two color B seed beads, go through the end two RAW beads (**photo a**). Go back through two Bs and make another two-bead square stitch to create a strip of four Bs. Continue in the two-bead square stitch (**photo b**) for 20 rows.

[2] When you finish the strip, secure it to the corresponding column on the opposite edge of the bracelet with square stitch. Secure the tail.

[3] Repeat steps 1 and 2 to make a strip over each widthwise column.

[4] Repeat step 1 to make five lengthwise strips using color C seed beads. Remember not to square stitch a bead to the single A beads added between the RAW stitches in step 2 of "Closure." Make these strips 95 rows long, but do not attach them to the base until all five are complete. Leave 12 in. (30cm) of thread at the end of each strip to secure the strips at the other end after weaving them through the widthwise strips.

Weave the strips together

[1] When the lengthwise strips are done, weave them over and under the widthwise strips (**photo c**).

[2] Because weaving takes up slack, you may have to add rows of square stitch to the ends. You can do this at any time. The strips should fit without pulling, but should not be baggy.

[3] When you finish weaving, attach each strip to the RAW base with the remaining thread. Secure the tails, and trim.

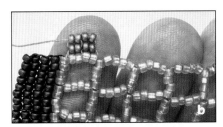

Beaded bead caps and beads

Build quick pyramids with seed beads to create fun, bubbly bead caps. Pyramid beads also can be stitched together side by side for a bracelet with unusual texture.

by **Tracy List**

Beaded bead cap

When working, it's important to keep thread tension fairly tight and consistent so that the cap isn't wobbly or loose. This may take some practice. If you have trouble in the beginning, try working each step in a different color, as shown in **photos a–c.**

The directions below make four-sided caps. Make five- or six-sided caps by stringing 10 or 12 beads in step 1.

[1] Thread a needle with 20 in. (51cm) of conditioned Nymo (see Techniques, p. 10). Pick up eight color A seed beads and tie a square knot (Techniques) to form a ring, leaving a 5-in. (13cm) tail. Seal the knot with G-S Hypo Cement.

[2] Pick up three As, skip a bead on the ring, and go through the next A (**figure 1, a–b**). Repeat to add three As between every other bead in the ring (**b–c**). Tie another square knot when you reach the tail. You will have four evenly spaced points around the circle.

[3] Step up through the first bead in the first three-bead point (**c–d**). Pick up one A and go through the third bead of the three-bead point (**figure 2, a–b**). Sew through the next bead and the first bead on the next three-bead point (**b–c**). Continue adding one A between

the first and third beads in each of the three-bead points made in the previous step. These beads sit on top of the points (**c–d** and **photo a,** yellow beads).

After adding the beads to each point, sew through the beads to exit the first bead of the original ring made in step 1, the bead to the left of where the tail exits (**d–e**).

[4] Beads #1, 3, 5, and 7 of the original ring are now in the center of the beadwork. Pick up one A and sew through bead #3 (**figure 3, a–b**). Continue adding a bead between the remaining beads of this center section (**b–c** and **photo b,** red beads).

[5] Sew through the first bead added in the previous step (**c–d**). Pick up an A and go through the next bead on the previous row. Continue around until this new row consists of four beads (**photo c,** black beads). Step up through the first bead of this row, and add one more row of four beads.

[6] Sew through the last row a few times to reinforce it, pulling the beads tightly in the center.

[7] To reinforce the other rows on the cap, sew down through the beads from the top corners to the bead in the middle of each side and up through the next top corner (**figure 4, point a**). Repeat around the cap.

[8] Next, anchor the corner beads on each point (added in step 3). Sew through the corner bead, the middle bead on the row, and the next corner bead (**figure 4, point b**). Continue around until all four-corner beads are secured. Weave back to the tail and tie the ends together with a square knot. Secure the tails by weaving into the beadwork and tying a few half-hitch knots (Techniques), and trim.

You now have a beaded bead cap. Use it just as is, stack it with some spacers made by working steps 1–2, or join caps together to make a pyramid bracelet (below). You can also make a beaded bead by repeating steps 3–8 on the other side of the base (steps 1–2).

Pyramid bracelet (p. 66)

When making the end bead caps, tie off the tails, but don't clip the thread. You'll use it to complete the loop and bead closure.

[1] Make 11 bead caps as described above, and set them aside while making the clasp end pyramids.

[2] Make a bead cap starting with 1 yd. (.9m) of conditioned thread.

MATERIALS

bracelet 7½ in. (19.1cm) (includes 13 bead cap pyramids)

- 8–10mm bead (for clasp)
- **16** 4mm beads
- **30** 2mm beads
- **16** 4mm accent beads
- Japanese seed or cylinder beads
  7g color A
  2g color B
- Nymo B, conditioned with beeswax
- beading needles, #12
- G-S Hypo Cement

a

b

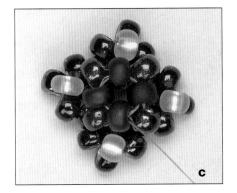

c

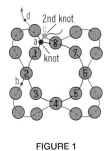

FIGURE 1

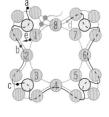

FIGURE 2

FIGURE 3

FIGURE 4

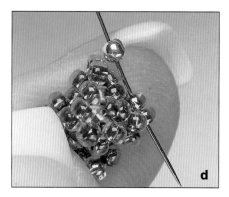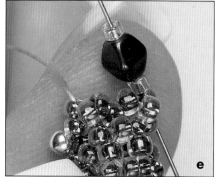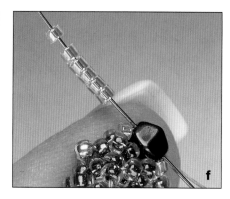

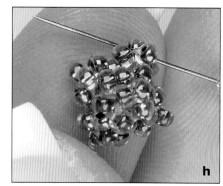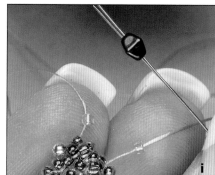

End with the working tail exiting the same spot as the original tail.

[3] Pick up one 2mm bead, and go through the first two beads on a three-bead point (photo d). Pick up a color B seed bead, a 4mm bead, and a B, and go through the point bead and the bead after it in the next three-bead point (photo e).

[4] Repeat step 3 to complete the ring. Then retrace the thread path to reinforce all the beads just added. End with the needle exiting the last 4mm added.

[5] Pick up six Bs, and go through the 4mm again in the same direction (photo f). Go through the first three Bs just added. Pick up the 8–10mm bead and an A. Go back through the

8–10mm and the last three Bs of the six added to begin this step (photo g). Retrace the thread path. Weave in the tails, tying several half-hitch knots between the beads, seal the knots with glue, and trim.

[6] Make a pyramid bead to use as the other half of the clasp as shown in step 3, but pick up the 4mm and enough As to fit around the clasp bead. Reinforce the thread path, and secure the thread as in the previous step.

[7] Thread a needle on each end of 1 yd. of thread. Center the thread through the 4mm bead opposite the loop on the end pyramid.

[8] On one needle, pick up a B, and go through a center point bead (photo h) and the bead after it on a new cap.

Pick up a 2mm and go through the next two beads so the needle exits the next center point bead. Repeat with the other needle on the other side of the pyramid. Pick up a B on each needle, then cross the needles through a 4mm (photo i). Repeat until all but the clasp pyramid is joined.

[9] To join the remaining clasp pyramid, pick up a B on each needle, and cross the needles through the 4mm bead on the clasp pyramid. Reinforce this join. Weave in the tails, secure them with half-hitch knots, glue, and trim.

Create ropes, laces, fabrics, and more by stitching seed beads using different patterns and techniques. From lush cording to airy lace, or glinting metal to rich tapestry, seed beads can be combined to look like almost any textile under the sun.

Channel bracelet

Simulate the look of fabricated metal jewelry in this square stitch bracelet. Hex-cut seed beads in a metallic finish complete the design.

by **Kate McKinnon**

[1] Pick up an 8º seed bead, two 11ºs, and an 8º on a comfortable length of waxed thread (see Techniques, p. 10). Turn, pick up two 11ºs, and square stitch (Techniques) them to the 8º in the previous row (**photo a**). Pick up an 8º, and stitch it to the two 11ºs in the center of the previous row. Pick up two 11ºs and stitch them to the 8º at the start of the previous row.
[2] Continue working an alternating pattern of 8ºs and 11ºs until the strip is 1½ in. (3.8cm) shorter than the desired bracelet length. End with a row that has the same bead sequence as the first row. Make a second strip identical to the first.
[3] With the thread exiting an end bead on the last row, string three 8ºs

and sew through the last row of the first strip (**photo b**). Turn, and sew through that strip's second-to-last row. Pick up three 8ºs, and sew through the second-to-last row of the second strip. Go back and square stitch together the newly added beads (**photo c**).
[4] When the two strips are connected, start adding crystals. Sew through the beadwork, exiting at the inside edge of the fourth row.
[5] Pick up a crystal, and continue through the corresponding row on the other strip (**photo d**). Turn, and work back through the nearby beads until you exit the same bead or beads that you entered on this strip. Go back through the crystal, and repeat on the

other side. Make four passes through the crystal to secure it. Work through the strip, exiting the fourth row from the first crystal.
[6] Repeat step 5 along the length of the bracelet.
[7] After you've added the last crystal, you may have to stitch a row or two to the strips so that the number of rows before the first crystal and after the last one are equal. Then string two rows of 8ºs between the last two rows on the strips as in step 3, and square stitch them together.
[8] Square stitch a row of 11ºs onto the bracelet's edge. Create a triangular finish by omitting the end pair of beads on each side of each row (**photo e**).

MATERIALS

bracelet 6½ in. (16.5cm)

- **12–17** 8mm round crystals
- **5** 6mm bicone crystals (optional)
- 5g size 11º Japanese cylinder beads
- 8g size 8º hex-cut Japanese cylinder beads
- lobster claw clasp
- 2 in. (5cm) chain (with links large enough to accommodate the lobster claw clasp) or 6mm soldered jump ring
- **7–14** 2-in. head pins (optional)
- Nymo B, conditioned with beeswax
- beading needles, #12
- chainnose pliers (optional)
- roundnose pliers (optional)
- wire cutters

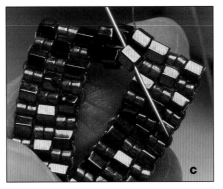

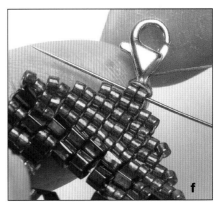

[9] Sew a lobster claw clasp onto the last row of the triangle (**photo f**). Retrace the thread path several times. Sew a soldered jump ring on the opposite end of the bracelet.

For an optional decorative finish: Sew a soldered jump ring onto the last row of the triangle. Retrace the thread path several times. Trim the end from a head pin and make the first half of a wrapped loop (Techniques). Attach it to the jump ring and complete the wraps. String an 8mm bead and make the first half of a wrapped loop. Attach the lobster claw clasp and complete the wraps. On the other end of the bracelet, sew on a small length of chain. String a crystal on a head pin, and make the first half of a wrapped loop. Attach the loop to a link of chain, finish the wraps, and trim. Repeat to add as many crystals as desired to the chain.

> **EDITOR'S NOTE:** This bracelet calls for using three 8ºs between strips, which equals the width of the 8mm crystals shown. If you want to use a different size or type of decorative bead, simply adjust the number of 8ºs to match the new bead's width.

Peyote-link chain

Peyote stitch creates a versatile fabric that can be formed into many shapes. Piece together a fun, three-dimensional peyote chain in varying hues for a unique necklace.

by **Sonja Podjan**

MATERIALS

20-link necklace 18 in. (46cm)

- 40g size 11º Japanese seed beads, **2–10** colors (2g for each link)
- toggle clasp
- C-Lon or Nymo D, conditioned with beeswax or Thread Heaven
- beading needles, #12
- clear nail polish or floor wax and a small paintbrush

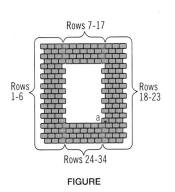

Rows 7-17
Rows 1-6
Rows 18-23
Rows 24-34
FIGURE

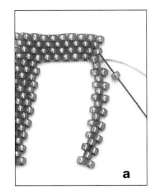

a

b

c

Refer to the pattern above as you work.
[1] String a stop bead (see Techniques, p. 10) to 8 in. (20cm) from the end of a 1-yd (.9m) length of conditioned thread (Techniques). Sew through the stop bead again.
[2] Pick up 20 beads and work flat, even-count peyote (Techniques) for six rows. This completes the first side of the link (rows 1–6).
[3] For side 2, stitch two beads per row for 11 rows (rows 7–17).
[4] For side 3, stitch two beads for two rows (rows 18–19). Then pick up 16 beads, and push them against the last bead on row 18. Work a row of peyote with the beads just strung, and the up beads from row 19 (**photo a**). Continue working in peyote until this side is six rows wide (rows 18–23).

[5] Weave back through the beads, and exit down through the third up bead from the bottom inside edge of side 3. See **point a** on the pattern.
[6] For side 4, work 11 two-bead rows as in step 3 to complete the last side of the link (rows 24–34).
[7] When you're ready to close a link, align the beads on row 34 with the beads on row 6. Zip up the edge beads (Techniques) to stitch the sides together. Secure the working thread with half-hitch knots (Techniques) between a few beads and trim the excess thread.
[8] To attach the clasp, remove the stop bead, and thread a needle on the tail. Pick up three beads, sew through the loop on a clasp half, and pick up three more beads. Sew through the bead the thread exits in the same

direction to form a ring (**photo b**). Sew through the beads again, secure the thread in the beadwork, and trim.
[9] Repeat steps 1–6 to make a second link.
[10] Connect the new link to the previous link (**photo c**). Repeat step 7. Remove the stop bead, secure the tail, and trim.
[11] Continue making and connecting links until you have a chain of 20 rectangles. Attach the remaining clasp half to the end link as you did in step 8.
[12] Lay the necklace as flat as possible. Apply a thin coat of floor wax with a paintbrush or use clear nail polish on the links to stiffen them. Let the links dry, then rearrange them so you can coat the parts of each link that were covered by other links. Let dry as before, and add a second coat if necessary.

OTHER TEXTILES

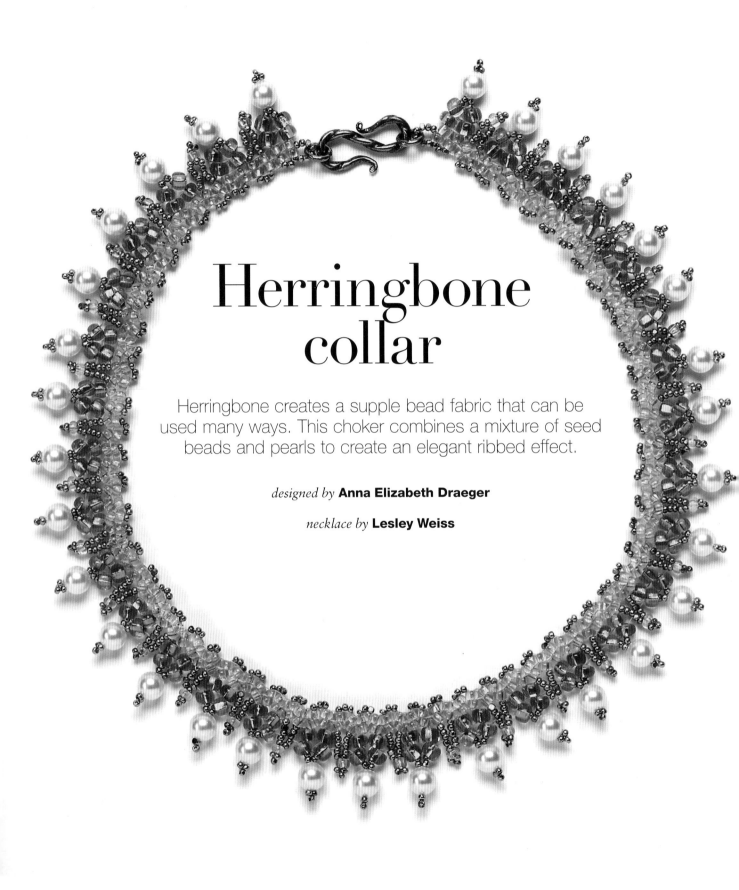

Herringbone collar

Herringbone creates a supple bead fabric that can be used many ways. This choker combines a mixture of seed beads and pearls to create an elegant ribbed effect.

designed by **Anna Elizabeth Draeger**

necklace by **Lesley Weiss**

MATERIALS

necklace 15½ in. (39.4cm)

- 10g size 8° seed beads, transparent light peach
- 8g size 6° seed beads, copper-lined
- hank size 13° Charlottes, copper-plated
- strand 6mm glass pearls
- S-hook clasp with two soldered jump rings, copper
- C-Lon or Nymo D, conditioned with beeswax or Thread Heaven
- beading needle, #13

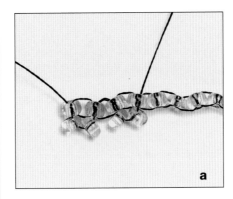

a

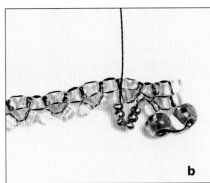

b

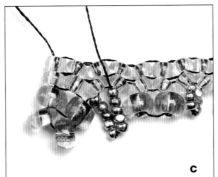

c

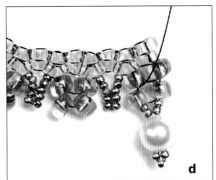

d

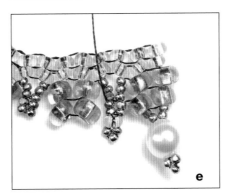

c

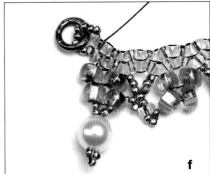

d

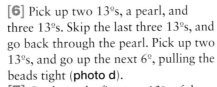

e

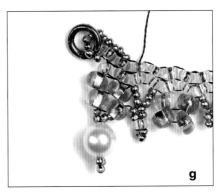

f

g

[1] Determine the finished length of your necklace. This one is 15½ in. (39.4cm). Subtract ½-in. (1.3cm) for the clasp.

[2] Thread a needle with a comfortable length of conditioned thread (see Techniques, p. 10). Leaving a 6-in. (15cm) tail, stitch a ladder (Techniques) of 8° seed beads the length determined in step 1. Your total number of beads must result in an odd number when divided by two. (This necklace has a ladder of 126 beads: 126 ÷ 2 = 63.)

[3] When your ladder is the desired length, begin herringbone stitch (Techniques), adding two 8°s with each stitch (photo a, black thread used for photo). Continue until you reach the end of the row. Your needle will be exiting the end ladder bead, facing away from the row of herringbone.

[4] To get in position to begin the next row, turn by going through the adjacent ladder bead, and continue through the last 8° added in the herringbone row. Pick up two 6°s, and go up the next 8°. Go down the next 8° and pick up six 13°s. Go up the 8° (photo b), and continue stitching in modified herringbone, alternating two 6°s on one stitch and six 13°s on the next stitch. End with a pair of 6°s, and turn as before to start the next row.

[5] Pick up two 6°s, and go up the next 6°. Go down the first three 13°s of the next stitch, pick up four 13°s, and go up the next three 13°s (photo c). Go down the next 6°. Continue stitching in modified herringbone, alternating two 6°s on one stitch and four 13°s on the next stitch. End with two 6°s, and turn as before to start the next row.

[6] Pick up two 13°s, a pearl, and three 13°s. Skip the last three 13°s, and go back through the pearl. Pick up two 13°s, and go up the next 6°, pulling the beads tight (photo d).

[7] Go down the first two 13°s of the next stitch. Pick up an 8° and three 13°s, and go back through the 8° and up the next two 13°s (photo e). Continue stitching, alternating pearls and 8°s, until you reach the end of the row.

[8] Weave through the base to exit the top of an end 6°. Pick up eight 13°s and a soldered jump ring, and go through the 6° again in the same direction (photo f). Retrace the thread path twice (the last time may be tight), exiting the 6° again.

[9] Pick up three 13°s, and go down the next 6°. Come up the next 6° (photo g) and repeat. Continue until

you reach the end of the row, and go down the last 6°.

[10] Pick up eight 13°s and the other ring for the clasp. Go down through the last 6° again, and retrace the thread path twice. Weave the tails into the beadwork, tying a few half-hitch knots (Techniques) between beads, and trim.

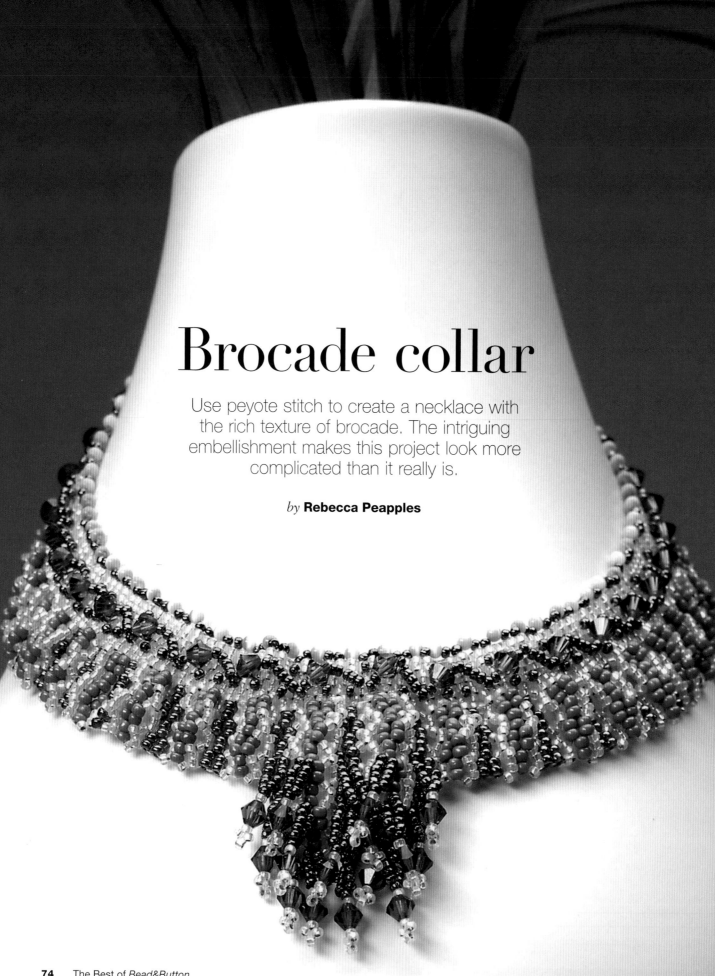

Brocade collar

Use peyote stitch to create a necklace with the rich texture of brocade. The intriguing embellishment makes this project look more complicated than it really is.

by **Rebecca Peapples**

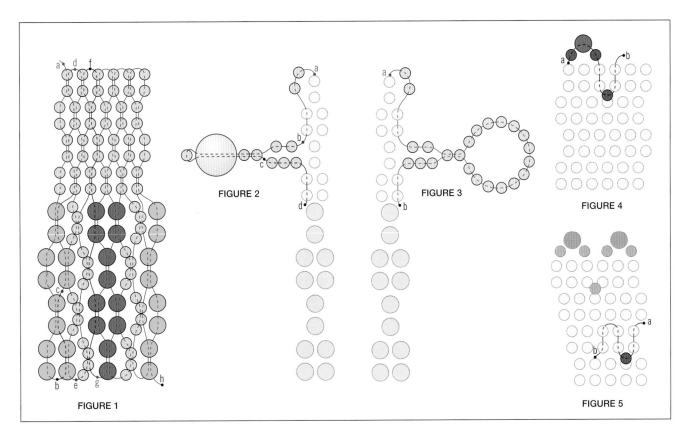

FIGURE 1

FIGURE 2

FIGURE 3

FIGURE 4

FIGURE 5

Necklace

Make the base in flat, two-drop peyote stitch, working top to bottom and left to right. Keep the tension comfortably tight to help maintain the ruffled bottom. When you run out of thread, weave the working thread into the stitches on the ruffled bottom so you don't block any of the 15ºs, which will be embellished later. Begin a new thread where the old one left off.

[1] On 3 yd. (2.7m) of conditioned thread (see Techniques, p. 10), pick up eight color A seed beads and eight Cs (**figure 1, a–b**), leaving a 12-in. (30cm) tail. These beads form rows 1 and 2.

Row 3: Work in two-drop peyote (Techniques): Pick up two Cs, skip two Cs on the previous row, and sew through the next two Cs (**b–c**). Work the next stitch with two Cs and the following two stitches with As (**c–d**).

Row 4: Two As, two As, four As, four As (**d–e**).

Row 5: Pick up four As. Sew through the second and third As on the last stitch of the previous row. Repeat once. Two As, two As (**e–f**).

Row 6: Two As, two As. Pick up two Ds. Sew through the second and third As on the previous row. Repeat once (**f–g**).

Rows 7–12: Continue working as shown (**g–h**).

[2] Repeat rows 3–12 to the desired length. You can stop in the middle of the necklace base if you want to add the optional centerpiece (p. 76), but complete the sequence so you end with row 12. Don't cut the thread.

Closure

[1] Thread a needle on the tail left in row 1. Pick up two As, skip two As in the end row, and sew through the next two As (**figure 2, a–b**).

[2] Pick up four As, the clasp bead, and an A. Sew back through the clasp bead and two As (**b–c**).

[3] Pick up three As and sew through the next two As on the end row (**c–d**). Retrace the thread path, secure the tail, and trim.

[4] Repeat step 1 with the working thread, then pick up four As plus enough As to make a loop large enough to fit over the clasp bead. Sew through the fourth and third As, pick up three As, and sew into the next two As on the end row (**figure 3, a–b**). Retrace the thread path, secure the tail, and trim.

Embellishment

[1] Start a new thread, and secure it in the base 15ºs, exiting at **figure 4, point a**.

[2] Pick up a B, a 2mm bead (or a C), and a B. Skip a row, and sew down through two As in the next base row. Pick up a B, and sew up two As in the next base row (**a–b**).

[3] Repeat step 2 until you reach the other end of the necklace. Secure the tails, and trim.

[4] Start a new thread, and exit at **figure 5, point a**. Sew down two 15ºs in the first row, and pick up a B. Sew up through two 15ºs in the next row and down through two 15ºs in the following row (**a–b**). Repeat until you reach the other end of the necklace, then secure the thread.

[5] Start a new thread, and exit the first B along the first row on the top of the base. Pick up five Bs, and sew through the third B along the second row of Bs (**photo a**). Pick up a B, a 4mm crystal, and a B. Sew through the third B on the top edge (**photo b**). Repeat across the necklace base.

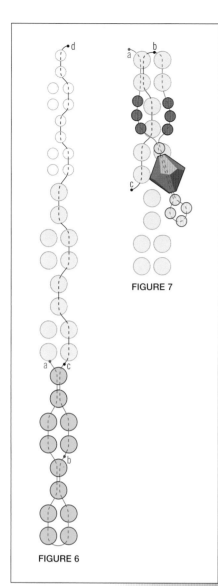

FIGURE 7

FIGURE 6

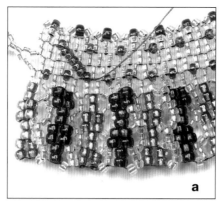

a

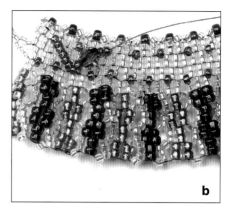

b

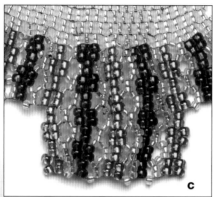

c

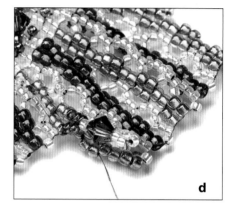

d

EDITOR'S NOTE: Since the bottom curves more than the top of the base, it is important to keep steady tension on the separation between the top half and the bottom. Otherwise, there will be gaps between the stitches.

Centerpiece (optional)

To work an increase in the center of the necklace, refer to figure 6.

[1] After row 12, pick up ten Cs. Skip two Cs, and sew through the next two Cs (a–b).

[2] Work the next stitch in Cs (b–c).

[3] Continue the centerpiece pattern (c–d), adding a total of 24 increase rows (photo c) and ending at point d. Then switch back to the base pattern to mirror the first half of the base.

Centerpiece embellishment (optional)

To embellish the rows of 11°s, pick up three As, a B, a crystal, and four Bs. Sew back up through a B, the crystal, and a B. Pick up three As and sew into the next two 11°s on the base (figure 7, a–b). Sew through six 11°s, exiting at point c (photo d). Repeat the bead sequence to make the next crystal fringe. Add as much fringe as desired.

MATERIALS

necklace 16 in. (41cm)

- 8–10mm bead for clasp
- **100** 4mm glass beads or crystals
- **120** 2mm round glass or gemstone beads
- Japanese seed beads
  15g size 11°, color C
  15g size 11°, color D
  20g size 15°, color A
  10g size 15°, color B
- Nymo D or B, conditioned with beeswax or Thread Heaven
- beading needles, #12 or #13

Stitch sampler necklace

Combine six techniques in this sparkling necklace featuring a bead-woven rope and a fringed medallion.

by **Judy Mullins**

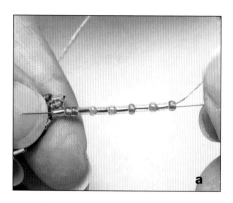

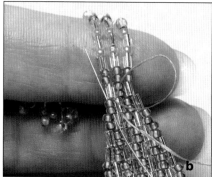

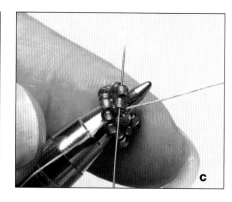

Pendant

[1] Make a ladder (see Techniques, p. 10) that alternates a pair of color A seed beads with a bugle bead 11 times. Go back through the ladder to reinforce it.

[2] Work in brick stitch (Techniques) following **figure 1** to make a triangle shape with a total of 20 rows. The last row should have three columns.

[3] With the needle exiting one of the bottom columns, begin fringing the pendant. Make all the fringes as shown in **figure 2**, and vary the seed bead colors in a way that pleases you. To make the first fringe, string all the beads, skip the last three seed beads, and go back up all the beads and the bugle that you exited on the pendant (**photo a**).

[4] Bring the needle down the adjacent seed bead pair, and make the second fringe like the first. Repeat on the bugle.

[5] To step up one row, bring the needle back up the bugle you exited and the bugle or seed bead pair one in from the edge of the next-to-last row. Come back down the edge bugle or pair of seed beads to begin the fringe (**photo b**).

MATERIALS

necklace 18 in. (46cm)

- **41** 3mm bicone crystals
- **41** 4mm bicone crystals
- 10g 3mm bugle beads, size #1
- 20g size 11º seed beads, color A
- 10g size 11º seed beads, in **1** or **2** colors, B and C
- clasp
- Nymo B or D, conditioned with beeswax or Thread Heaven
- beading needles, #12 or 13

Continue stepping up one row at a time along the first side. After making the last fringe on the side, weave the thread into the beadwork, securely tying a few half-hitch knots (Techniques) between beads. Weave through a few beads after the last knot, and trim.

[6] Attach a new thread securely near the bottom of the pendant on the other side and exit the edge bead of the next-to-last row. Fringe this side like the first.

Neck band

[1] Pick up 16 color A 11º seed beads (or an alternating pattern of As and Bs) and tie the beads into a ring using a surgeon's knot (Techniques). Sew through the next bead after the knot. Pick up three seed beads, skip three beads on the ring, and sew through the fourth bead (**figure 3, a–b**). Continue adding beads in this fashion until you sew through the first bead on the ring again (**b–c**). Until you have a few rows to hold onto, place the tube on a pen tip or narrow dowel (**photo c**).

[2] To step up to begin the next row, go through the first two beads added in the last row (**c–d**). Pick up three beads, and go through the center bead of the next three-bead group (**d–e**). Repeat around, stepping up to begin the third row (**e–f**). Work tubular netting until you reach the center of the neck band where the pendant will hang.

[3] With your thread exiting the middle bead of a three-bead group, pick up one bead and sew through the middle bead of the next three-bead group (**figure 4, a–b**). Repeat around to add a total of four beads. Step up through the first bead added in this round (**b–c**). Continue to work

in even-count tubular peyote stitch (Techniques) for the width of the pendant top plus a few rows. Then resume stitching tubular netting as shown in **figure 5**, picking up three beads between each peyote stitch.

[4] When the tube is about 1½ in. (3.8cm) short of the desired length, switch back to peyote stitch for about ½ in. (1.3cm). Secure the tail and trim. Stitch ½ in. of peyote at the other end of the tube.

[5] Embellish the tubular netting as shown in **figure 6**: Attach a new thread at the end of the tube, and bring it out a side bead on one of the open diamonds in the first row, pointing away from the end. Pick up a color B or C 11º seed bead, and sew through the side bead on the next diamond diagonally below (**a–b**). Repeat around, spiraling from one diamond to the next (**photo d**).

Pendant hanger and clasp

[1] Secure a new thread to the top left-hand corner of the pendant, and pick up the number of seed beads it takes to go around the neck tube loosely.

[2] Make three rows of square stitch (Techniques), using this strand of beads as the base.

[3] Sew back down the middle row to the pendant and connect the completed strip to the top of the pendant (**photo e**). After attaching the third row, sew through the row to the other end of the strip.

[4] Loop the strip over the neck band, and connect it behind the pendant in the same manner (**photo f**).

[5] Repeat steps 1–4 on the other side.

[6] Finally, sew the clasp securely to each end of the necklace.

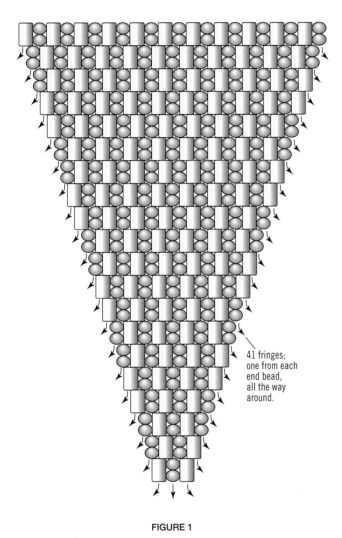

41 fringes;
one from each
end bead,
all the way
around.

FIGURE 1

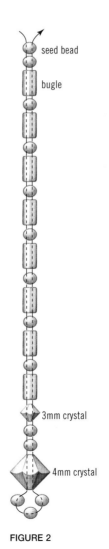

seed bead

bugle

3mm crystal

4mm crystal

FIGURE 2

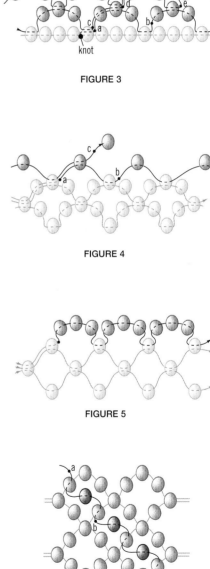

FIGURE 3

knot

FIGURE 4

FIGURE 5

FIGURE 6

OTHER TEXTILES

Helix swirl bracelet

Spirals of gold seem to wrap around colorful rings in these helix stitch bracelets.
Peyote stitch tubes provide the perfect finish.

by **Nancy Zellers**

a

b

c

[1] Working with a 4-ft. (1.2m) length of conditioned doubled thread (see Techniques, p. 10), string three color A beads and one color B bead. Repeat three times for a total of 16 beads.
[2] Leaving an 8-in. (20cm) tail, tie the beads into a ring around a dowel with a surgeon's knot (Techniques). Make sure the knot is facing you and that there are three As to the left of the knot.

[3] Pick up three As and two Bs. Working to the left, sew down behind the thread on the ring between the third and fourth beads (**photo a**).
[4] Pull on the thread, holding the beads in place with your finger. Keep the tension tight as you work, especially for the first inch (2.5cm).
[5] Pick up three As and two Bs and sew down behind the bead ring

between the seventh and eighth beads on the ring (**photo b**). Hold the loop in place with your finger as you did before. Repeat around the ring.
[6] On the remaining rounds, sew down between the third and fourth beads (A and first B) on the previous round as you did before (**photo c**). The Bs will begin to spiral around the dowel (**photo d**).

d

e

f

[7] Continue until you reach the desired length. These bracelets are 7½–8 in. (19.1–20cm) long.

[8] Remove the tube from the dowel. Bring the ends of the bracelet together, align the spiral pattern, and sew them together (**photo e**). Secure the tails with half-hitch knots (Techniques) between beads and trim the excess thread.

[9] On a new 1-yd. (.9m) length of thread, string a stop bead (Techniques), leaving an 8-in. tail. Go through the bead again in the same direction.

[10] Work in even-count, flat peyote (Techniques) following a pattern shown below. The finished peyote strip is ten beads wide and 36 rows long.

[11] Wrap the peyote strip around the bracelet where the ends meet and zip up the ends of the strip (Techniques) to form a tube (**photo f**).

[12] Secure the thread in the peyote tube. Sew the tube to the bracelet so it stays in place.

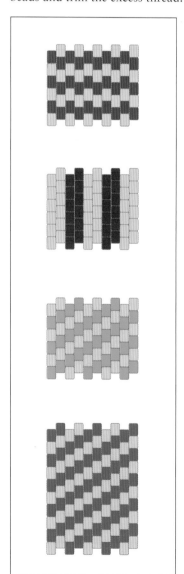

EDITOR'S NOTE: Tape the tail to the dowel above the ring to keep it out of the way and secure the ring in place.

To add a new thread, tape the working thread to the dowel, start the new thread, and sew through the beads on the previous row, tying half-hitch knots between a few beads. Exit the second B on the last loop, sew under the thread bridge, and continue working as before. Secure the old thread by sewing through a diagonal of Bs and tying half-hitch knots.

MATERIALS
bracelet 7½–8 in. (19.1–20cm)
- size 11º seed beads
  12g color A
  8g color B
- Nymo D, conditioned with beeswax
- beading needles, #10
- wood dowel with a ¼-in. (6mm) diameter

Netted stars

Make a handful of twinkling lace stars, then
stitch them together for a sparkling pendant.

by **Mindi Hawman**

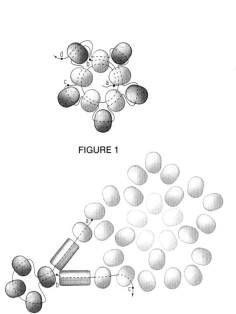

FIGURE 1

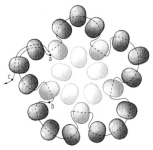

FIGURE 2

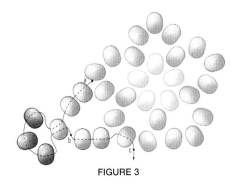

FIGURE 3

FIGURE 4

Make the star

[1] Thread a needle with 2 ft. (61cm) of conditioned Nymo (see Techniques, p. 10). Pick up five 11º color A seed beads, and go back through all five again, tightening the beads into a ring and leaving a 3 in. (7.6cm) tail. Sew through two more beads, holding the tail to keep the tension snug (figure 1, a–b).

[2] Pick up a color B seed bead and sew through the next A on the ring (b–c). Repeat around the ring, adding a B between each bead. Step up through the first bead added in this step (c–d).

MATERIALS

all projects
- Nymo D, conditioned with beeswax or Thread Heaven
- beading needles, #12
- G-S Hypo Cement

one star
- 1g size 11º seed beads, in each of **3–4** colors
- 2g 2–4mm bugle beads (optional)
- Future floor wax (optional)

necklace 18–22 in. (46–56cm)
- 10g size 11º seed beads
- clasp
- 2 bead tips

[3] Pick up three Cs and sew through the next B (figure 2, a–b). Continue around, adding three Cs between each of the Bs. Step up through the middle C of the first three beads added in this step (b–c).

[4] There are two variations for adding the star's points:
- Pick up three As and three Ds, and sew back through the third A picked up (figure 3, a–b). Keep the tension snug. Pick up two more As and sew through the middle bead on the next three-bead group (b–c). Add four more points to complete the star.
- Pick up an A, a bugle bead, and four Bs. Go back through the first B after the bugle (figure 4, a–b). Pick up a bugle bead and an A and go through the middle bead on the next three-bead group. Repeat around to add four more points.

[5] Sew back through the beadwork to the tail. Without removing the needle, tie the working thread and tail with a surgeon's knot (Techniques). Dab the knot with glue, and sew through a few beads with the working thread. Tug the knot into a bead, and trim the threads close to the beads.

[6] To stiffen the star, dip the star into Future floor wax. Blot it with a paper towel, and let it dry.

Assemble the necklace

[1] Repeat steps 1–5 of "Make the star" to make a total of six stars.

[2] Secure a new thread in a star.

[3] Sew through the beadwork to exit a point bead. Sew into the point bead of another star, and back into the point on the first star. Retrace the thread path.

[4] Repeat step 3 to attach all the stars together as in the photo on p. 83.

[5] Center a needle on a 2-yd. (1.8m) length of conditioned thread.

[6] Sew through a corner point bead in the top row of stars. Center the star on the thread.

[7] String approximately 8–10 in. (20–25cm) of seed beads on the doubled thread. Sew into a bead tip from the outside.

[8] String a seed bead, and sew back through the bead tip and into the strand of seed beads. Secure the tail, and trim.

[9] Attach the needle to the other two threads, and string seed beads to the same length as step 7. Sew into the bead tip and seed bead from the first strand.

[10] Sew back through the bead tip, secure the tail in the strand, and trim.

[11] Open the loop on the bead tip, and attach it to one clasp half.

[12] Repeat steps 5–11 on the other side of the necklace.

Pineapple lace necklace

Weave an
intricate, lacy collar
featuring a classic
needlework motif.

by **Mary Anne Russell**

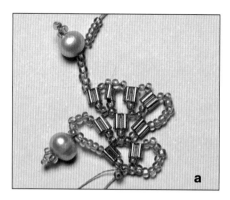

a

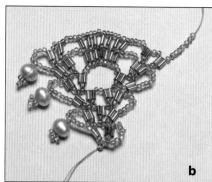

b

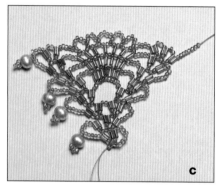

c

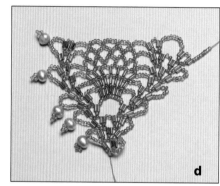

d

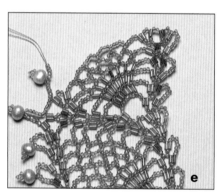

e

f

The pineapple is a traditional design symbolizing hospitality and welcome, and is commonly found in lacework patterns. To explain how to recreate the pattern in beads, we've used some unusual terminology. Don't let this intimidate you. Learn the terms as you use them in the project, and you'll quickly grow accustomed to them.

Necklace sides

Row 1: Center a needle on a 2-yd. (1.8m) length of conditioned thread (see Techniques, p. 10). Attach a stop bead (Techniques) 8–10 in. (20–25cm) from the end, and pick up eleven 11º seed beads. Make a large bead shell: Pick up two bugle beads, and go back through the first one in the same direction (**figure 1, a–b**). Pick up an 11º, and go through the second 11º

picked up to begin this row (**b–c**). Go back through the 11º just picked up and the second bugle picked up (**c–d**). Pick up three 11ºs and two bugles, and go back through the first bugle just picked up (**d–e**). Pick up an 11º, go through the first 11º picked up to begin this row, go back through the 11º just picked up, and continue through the last bugle picked up (**e–f**).

Make a pearl dangle: Pick up six 11ºs, a pearl, and three 11ºs, and go back through the pearl in the opposite direction (**figure 2, a–b**). Go through the sixth 11º pick up in the same direction as before (**b–c**), and pick up five 11ºs (**c–d**). Flip your work to begin the next row.

Row 2: Make a two-bugle cluster at the top of the large bead shell in the previous row: Pick up two bugles, and

go through the first bugle again in the same direction (**figure 3, a–b**). Pick up an 11º, go through the first 11º in the top of the large bead shell, and go back through the 11º just picked up (**b–c**). Continue through the last bugle added (**c–d**).

Pick up two 11ºs, and make a cluster in the next 11º in the large bead shell of the previous row. Repeat.

Pick up eight 11ºs. Flip your work.

Row 3: Make a cluster (**figure 3**) in each of the four 11ºs between the clusters of the previous row, picking up two 11ºs between each cluster. Make a pearl dangle (**figure 2** and **photo a**). Flip your work.

Row 4: Make a small bead shell in the two 11ºs between the first two clusters on the previous row (**figure 4**). The small bead shell has only two 11ºs between the bugle bead groups whereas the large bead shell has three 11ºs.

Pick up eleven 11ºs. Skip the middle two 11ºs between the clusters on the previous row. Make a small bead shell in the two 11ºs between the last two clusters on the previous row. Pick up eight 11ºs. Flip your work.

Row 5: Make a small bead shell (**figure 4**) in the shell of the previous row. Pick up six 11ºs and a bugle. Attach the bugle to the third 11º of the 11-bead loop in the row below (**figure 5, a–b**). Pick up an 11º and a bugle, and attach it to the next 11º below (**b–c**). Repeat until you've added seven bugles. Pick up five 11ºs. Make a small bead shell in the shell below. Make a pearl dangle. Flip your work.

Row 6: Make a small bead shell in the shell below. Pick up six 11ºs and a bugle. Attach the bugle in the seed bead above the first bugle in the row below as in **figure 5**. Pick up two 11ºs and a bugle, and attach to the 11º above the next bugle. Continue until you've added seven bugles. There should be one 11º between the 11ºs atop each bugle. Pick up five 11ºs, make a small bead shell in the shell below, and pick up eight 11ºs. Flip your work (**photo b**).

Row 7: Make a large bead shell (**figure 1**) in the small shell below. Pick up five 11ºs and a bugle. Go

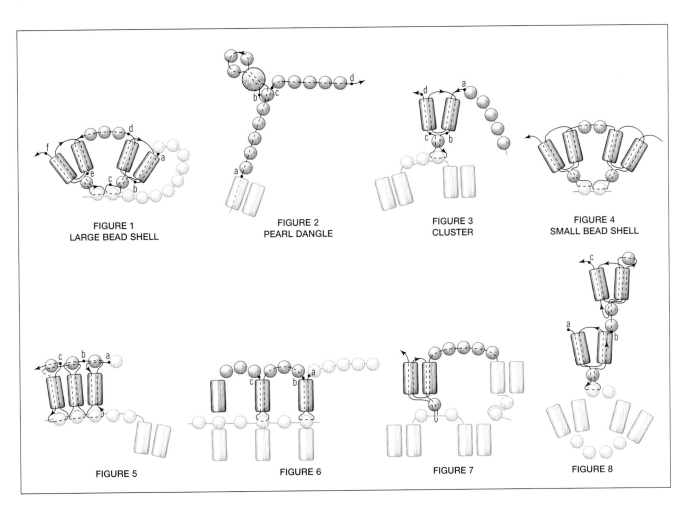

FIGURE 1
LARGE BEAD SHELL

FIGURE 2
PEARL DANGLE

FIGURE 3
CLUSTER

FIGURE 4
SMALL BEAD SHELL

FIGURE 5

FIGURE 6

FIGURE 7

FIGURE 8

through the 11º above the first bugle in the row, and go back through the bugle (**figure 6, a–b**). Pick up three 11ºs and a bugle, and repeat (**b–c**). Continue until you've added seven bugles. Pick up five 11ºs. Make a small bead shell (**figure 4**) in the shell below. Make a pearl dangle. Flip your work.

Row 8: Make a small bead shell in the shell below. *Pick up six 11ºs, go through the center 11º between the first two bugles below, and come back up the sixth 11º.* Repeat *–* five times. Pick up five 11ºs and

MATERIALS
necklace, 21 in. (53cm)
- **56** 5mm round pearls
- **2** hanks size 11º seed beads
- **2** hanks or 30g 5mm bugle beads
- clasp
- Nymo D, conditioned with beeswax or Silamide
- beading needles, #13
- G-S Hypo Cement

make three clusters (**figure 3**) in the large bead shell below with two 11ºs between the clusters. Pick up eight 11ºs. Flip your work (**photo c**).

Row 9: Make a small bead shell, pick up two 11ºs, and make another small bead shell between the clusters on the previous row. Pick up six 11ºs, and attach to the middle bead of the loop below as in row 8. Repeat four times. Pick up five 11ºs, make a small bead shell in the shell below, and make a pearl dangle. Flip your work.

Row 10: Make a small bead shell in the shell below. Pick up six 11ºs, and attach as before in the center bead of the loop below. Repeat three times. Pick up five 11ºs, make a small bead shell in the shell below, and pick up nine 11ºs (Note: this is the base of the next pineapple motif). Skip two 11ºs below, and make a small bead shell in the shell below. Pick up eight 11ºs. Flip your work (**photo d**).

Row 11: Make a small bead shell in the shell below. Pick up six 11ºs. Add seven bugles and seed beads as in

row 5 (**figure 5**). Pick up five 11ºs and make a small bead shell in the shell below. Pick up six 11ºs and attach as before in the center bead of each loop below. Repeat twice. Pick up five 11ºs, make a small bead shell in the shell below, make a pearl dangle, and flip your work.

Row 12: Make a small bead shell in the shell below. Pick up six 11ºs, and attach as before in the center bead of each loop below. Repeat once. Pick up five 11ºs, and make a small bead shell in the shell below. Pick up six 11ºs. Add seven bugles and seed beads as in row 6. Pick up five 11ºs, make a small bead shell in the shell below, and pick up eight 11ºs. Flip your work.

Row 13: Make a large bead shell (**figure 1**) in the small shell below. Pick up five 11ºs and a bugle. Go through the 11º above the bugle below, and go back through the bugle (**figure 6, a–b**). Pick up three 11ºs and a bugle, and repeat (**b–c**). Continue until you've added seven bugles. Pick up five 11ºs. Make a large bead shell (**figure 1**).

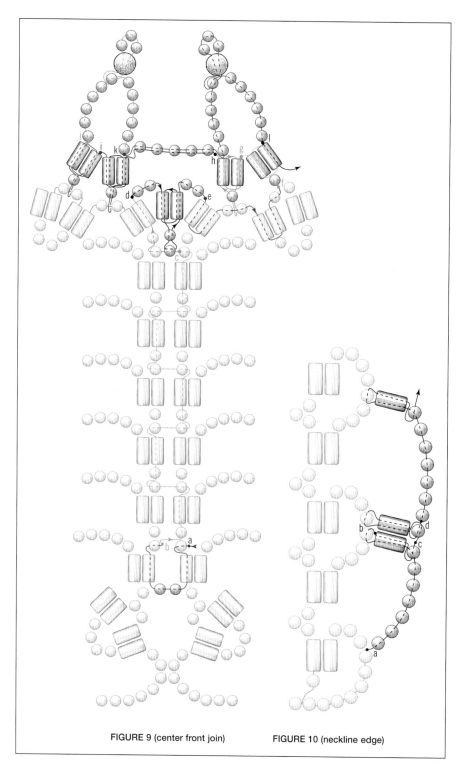

FIGURE 9 (center front join)   FIGURE 10 (neckline edge)

the clusters on the previous row. Pick up six 11ºs, go through the center 11º between the first two bugles below, and come back up through the sixth 11º. Repeat four times. Pick up five 11ºs. Make a small bead shell between the first two clusters. Pick up five 11ºs. Make a cluster, and attach it between the 11ºs between the second and third clusters on the previous row (**figure 7**). Without picking up any seed beads, make another cluster, and attach it between the 11ºs of the small shell on the row below as in **figure 7**. Make a pearl dangle, but pick up six 11ºs after the pearl instead of five. Go back through the five 11ºs between the second-to-last cluster and the last small shell. Make a regular pearl dangle (**photo e**).

Repeat steps 10–15 until you have completed four and a half pineapples. Then repeat rows 10–12.

Extension rows

Row 1: Make a small bead shell in the shell of the previous row. Continue with row 13 to the end of the row.
Row 2: Make a small bead shell in the shell below. Pick up two 11ºs, and make three clusters with two 11ºs between each in the bead shell below. Work row 14 *–*. Then pick up five 11ºs and make a cluster in the first 11º of the small shell below (**figure 8, a–b**). Pick up two 11ºs, and make a cluster as in **figure 8, b–c**. Flip your work.
Row 3: Pick up six 11ºs and attach to

Pick up six 11ºs, and attach as before to the center bead of the loop below. Pick up five 11ºs, make a small bead shell in the shell below, and make a pearl dangle. Flip your work.
Row 14: Make a small shell in the shell below. Pick up two 11ºs, and make three clusters (**figure 3**) with two 11ºs between each in the large bead shell below. *Pick up six 11ºs,

go through the center 11º between the first two bugles below, and come back though the sixth 11º.* Repeat *–* five times. Pick up five 11ºs, and make three clusters (**figure 3**) in the large bead shell below, adding two 11ºs between the clusters.
Row 15: Make a small bead shell, pick up two 11ºs, and make another small bead shell (**figure 4**) between

the center bead of the loop below as before five times. Pick up five 11ºs. Make a small bead shell between the first two clusters. Pick up five 11ºs. Make a cluster, and join it between the 11ºs of the second and third clusters as in **figure 7**. Make another cluster joined between the 11ºs of the small shell below as in row 15. Make a pearl dangle with six 11ºs after the pearl. Go back through the five 11ºs and make a regular pearl dangle.

Row 4: Begin as in row 10 of "Necklace side." After the bead loops, pick up five 11ºs. Make a cluster in the 11º atop the cluster of the row below. Pick up two 11ºs and make another cluster as in **figure 8**. Flip your work.

Row 5: Pick up six 11ºs, and attach to the top of the loop below. Repeat twice. Pick up five 11ºs. Make a small shell in the shell below. Make a pearl dangle and flip your work.

Row 6: Make a small shell in the shell below. Pick up six 11ºs, and attach to the center of the loops as before. Repeat once. Pick up five 11ºs and make a cluster in the 11º of the cluster below. Pick up two 11ºs and make a cluster as in **figure 8**. Flip your work.

Row 7: Pick up six 11ºs and attach to the center of the loop below. Pick up five 11ºs and make a small bead shell in the shell below. Make a pearl dangle.

Row 8: Make a small bead shell in the shell below. Pick up two 11ºs. Make a cluster in the cluster of

the previous row, and secure the thread with a few half-hitch knots (Techniques) between beads. This is the first half of the necklace. Make another identical half.

Center joining

[1] Lay the two halves of the necklace out with the two last pineapples of each side sitting side by side. Secure a new thread in one side and weave through the beadwork to exit at **figure 9, point a** (the 11º atop the first edge cluster in **figure 8**) (**photo f**). Go down the edge bugle, pick up two 11ºs, and come up the corresponding edge bugle and first 11º on the other side (**figure 9, a–b**). Following the thread path in **figure 9**, join the next four pairs of edge bugles and 11ºs without adding beads (**b–c**).

[2] After exiting the sixth edge bugle and 11º on the first side, pick up an 11º, and go up the 11ºs and the seventh edge bugle above the sixth edge bugle on the other side (**c–d**).

[3] Pick up two 11ºs, make a cluster, and pick up two 11ºs (**d–e**). Go through the beads along the first edge to exit the first 11º of the small bead shell (**e–f**).

[4] Pick up an 11º and make a ladder stitch (Techniques), exiting the first bugle (**f–g**).

[5] Make a cluster, and attach as shown (**g–h**). Pick up five 11ºs and make a cluster on the other side (**h–i**).

[6] Make another cluster (**i–j**), then a pearl dangle with six seeds in the second half (**j–k**).

[7] Go back through the five 11ºs and make a final pearl cluster with six 11ºs in the second half (**k–l**). Secure the thread, and trim.

Neckline shaping

[1] Secure a new thread in the first row at one end, and exit after the eighth 11º of the inside edge. Pick up seven 11ºs and a bugle, and go through the fourth 11º of the first eight-bead loop (**figure 10, a–b**). Go back up the bugle and through the last 11º in the same direction (**b–c**). Pick up an 11º and a bugle, and attach the same way to the next 11º of the loop (**c–d**).

[2] Continue attaching two bugles to the two center beads of each loop on the first side (17 more), picking up the following number of 11ºs between the loops: seven, seven, eight, 11, 11, 11, 11, 11, 11, ten, ten, nine, ten, ten, ten, seven, seven. You may need to adjust counts for a smooth edge.

[3] After attaching the second bugle to the last loop on the first side, do not add any 11ºs. Join the first loop on the second side with bugles and 11ºs so the center front meets in a "V." Resume the attachment pattern in reverse.

[4] Secure the thread in the same place on the final 11-bead loop. Then turn the work, and retrace the thread path along the neckline edge for additional strength.

[5] Finally, remove the stop bead and add the clasp using the starting tails.

> **EDITOR'S NOTE:**
> Because bugle beads have sharp edges, use waxed, doubled thread throughout. If possible, use Japanese bugles (not on hanks); their edges are smoother. If you use 3mm bugles, make an extra motif or two per side.

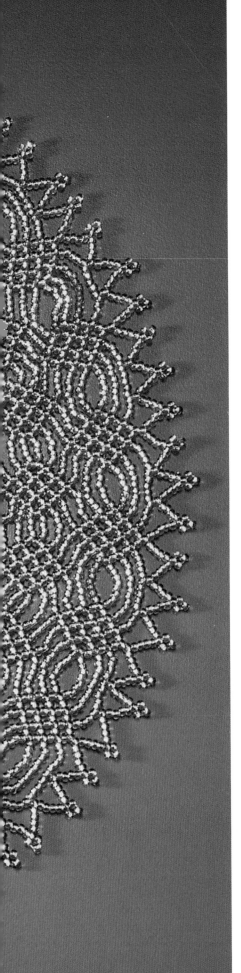

Ecuadorian lace weaves

Learn the traditional lace-making techniques of the Saraguro to make a beautiful lace collar or a pretty leaf bracelet.

by **Kelly Lightner** *and* **Alice Korach**

Araña necklace

[1] Thread a needle on a 1½-yd. (1.35m) length of doubled Stringth. String enough size 10º seed beads to go around the base of your neck. The total must be a number divisible by eight, plus two beads. This necklace base has 194 beads (194 - 2 = 192, 192 ÷ 8 = 24).

[2] Thread a needle with a comfortable length of conditioned Nymo (see Techniques, p. 10) and, leaving a 12–18 in. (30–46cm) tail, tie it together with the base cord against the last bead on one end, using an overhand knot (Techniques). On the other end of the base strand, temporarily hold the beads in place with a piece of tape, leaving a 12–18-in. tail.

MATERIALS
both projects
- Nymo D or F, conditioned with beeswax or Thread Heaven
- beading needles, #12

Araña necklace 17½ in. (44.5cm)
- **3** hanks size 10º seed beads
- **2** yd. (1.8m) Stringth, size #2

leaf bracelet 7 in. (18cm)
- 10g size 10º triangle beads
- shank button

Weaving

Row 1: Pick up ten beads. *Skip eight beads on the base, loop the thread from back to front around the base, and go through the last bead picked up (this will be referred to as a double-pass bead) (**figure 1, a–b**). Pick up nine beads (**b–c**).* Repeat *–* across the row. When only two beads remain on the base strand, pick up two beads, loop around the base strand after the last bead, and go through the last bead picked up (**d–e**).

Row 2: Pick up four beads and loop around the base cord after the fourth bead on row 1. Go through the last bead added (**e–f**). *Pick up seven beads, and loop around row 1 one bead before the next double-pass bead. Go through the last bead, pick up three beads, and go around row 1 one bead after the double-pass bead. Go through the last bead (**f–g**).* Repeat *–* across the row. Pick up three beads, go up the first bead of row 1, around the base cord, and back down the first bead of row 1 and the last two beads of row 2 (**h–i/a**).

Row 3: Pick up four beads, go around row 2 one bead after the last regular double-pass bead, and go back through the last bead. *Pick up five beads, and go around row 2 one bead before the next double-pass bead (**a–b**). Make two three-bead groups as shown (**b–c**).* Repeat *–* across the row. Join the last three-bead group by going through the first bead of row 2, around row 1, and back down the row 2 bead and the last two beads of row 3 (**d–e**).

Row 4: Pick up four beads, and go around the thread in the center of the next-to-last three-bead group of row 3 (**e–f**). Make three-bead groups across the row, skipping two beads on the row above each time (not counting double-pass beads) (**f–g–h–i–j**). To end, pick up three beads, go through the first bead of row 3, around row 2, and down the row 3 bead and the last two beads of row 4 (**j–k/a**).

Row 5: Start as row 3 (**a–b**). *Pick up five beads, skip a three-bead group on row 4, and go around the middle of the next group (**b–c**). Work two three-bead groups (**c–d**).* Repeat *–* across the row. End the last three-bead group by going up the last edge bead on the left-hand edge, around row 3, and down the edge bead and the last two beads added (**e–f**).

Row 6: Pick up five beads, and go around the middle of the next-to-last three-bead group of row 5 (**f–g**). *Pick up nine beads, and go around the middle of the next three-bead group. Make a three-bead group in the next three-bead group (**g–h**).* Repeat *–* across the row. After the last nine-bead group, pick up four beads, go up the last edge bead on the right-hand edge, and around row 4 (**i–j**). Go back down the edge bead and the last three beads picked up (**j–k/a**).

Row 7: Pick up seven beads, and go around the middle of the last nine-bead group in the row above (**a–b**). Make six-bead groups across the row as shown (**b–c–d–e**). To end, pick up four beads, go up the last two edge beads, around row 5, and back down the two edge beads and the last three beads picked up (**e–f**).

Row 8: Pick up eight beads, and go around row 7 one bead before the next-to-last double-pass bead. *Pick up three beads, skip two, pick up nine, skip eight (**g–h**).* Repeat *–* across the row. After the last three-bead group, pick up six beads, go up the last edge bead on the right, around row 6, and down the edge

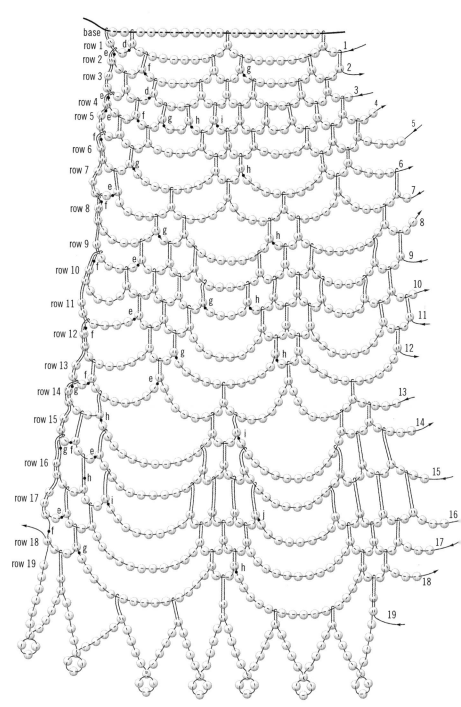

FIGURE 1 LEFT-HAND SIDE

bead and the last two beads picked up (**i–j/a**).

Row 9: Pick up seven beads, and go around row 8 one bead before the last three-bead group (**a–b**). *Make two three-bead groups (**b–c**), and pick up seven beads (**c–d**).* Repeat *–* across the row. After the last two three-bead groups, pick up five beads, go up the last two edge beads, around row 7, and back down the two edge beads and the last bead picked up (**e–f**).

Row 10: Pick up seven beads. *Make three three-bead groups (**f–g**). Pick up five beads (**g–h**).* Repeat *–* across the row. After the last three-bead group, pick up four beads, go up the last two edge beads, around row 8, and down the two edge beads and the last two beads picked up (**i–j/a**).

Row 11: Pick up eight beads (**a–b**). *Make two three-bead groups (**b–c**). Pick up nine beads (**c–d**).* Repeat *–* across the row. After the last two three-

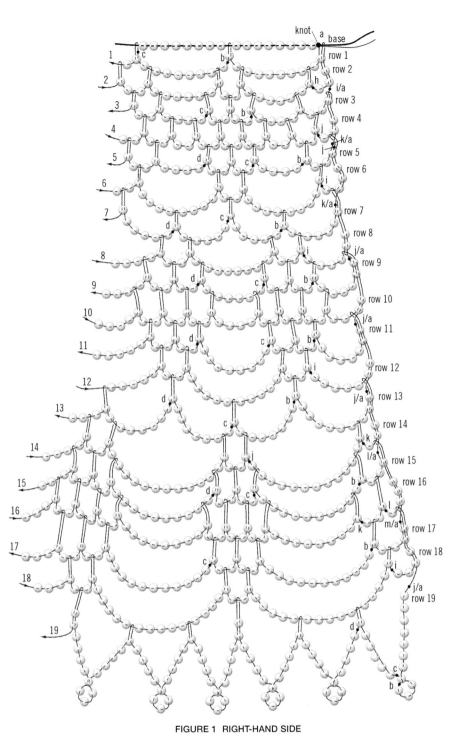

FIGURE 1 RIGHT-HAND SIDE

up 13 beads, then make a three-bead group (**h–i**).* Repeat *–* across the row. Connect the last 13-bead group as shown (**j–k**). Pick up three beads, go up the last two edge beads, around row 12, and down the two edge beads and the last two beads picked up (**j–k/a**).

Row 15: Pick up four beads, and loop around row 14 as shown (**a–b**). *Pick up 11 beads and loop around row 14 as shown (**b–c**). Make two three-bead groups (**c–d**).* Repeat *–* across the row. After the last 11-bead group, make a three-bead group and loop it around row 14 as shown (**e–f**). To end, pick up three beads, go up the last two edge beads, around row 13, and down the two edge beads and the last two beads picked up (**f–g**).

Row 16: Pick up five beads and loop around row 15 as shown (**g–h**). Make a three-bead group (**h–i**). *Pick up nine beads, and make three three-bead groups (**i–j**).* Repeat *–* across the row. After the last nine-bead group, make one three-bead group (**k–l**). Pick up four beads, go up the last edge bead, around row 14, and down the edge bead and the last three beads picked up (**l–m/a**).

Row 17: Pick up five beads, and loop around the middle of the last three-bead group in row 16 (**a–b**). *Pick up 12 beads, then make two three-bead groups (**b–c**)*. Repeat *–* across the row. After the last 12-bead group, make a three-bead group (**d–e**). Pick up four beads, go up the last two edge beads, around row 15, and down the two edge beads and the last three beads picked up (**e–f**).

Row 18: Pick up four beads, and go around the middle of the last three-bead group above (**f–g**). *Pick up 15 beads, then make a three-bead group (**g–h**).* Repeat *–* across the row. After the last 15-bead group, pick up four beads, go up the last two edge beads, around row 16, and down the two edge beads and the last two beads picked up (**i–j/a**).

Row 19: Pick up 11 beads (**a–b**). Go back through the eighth bead toward the start to make a picot (**b–c**). Pick up six beads, and loop around row 18 as shown (**c–d**).

bead groups, pick up six beads, go up the last two edge beads, around row 9, and go down the two edge beads and the last two beads picked up (**e–f**).

Row 12: Pick up nine beads. *Make a three-bead group (**f–g**). Pick up 11 beads (**g–h**).* Repeat *–* across the row. After the last three-bead group, pick up seven beads, go up the last two edge beads, around row 10, and down the two edge beads and the last two beads picked up (**i–j/a**).

Row 13: Pick up ten beads, and go around the middle of the last three-bead group on row 12 (**a–b**). Pick up eight-bead groups across the row (**b–c–d–e**). Connect the last eight-bead group as shown (**e–f**). To end, pick up three beads, go up the last two edge beads, around row 11, and down the two edge beads and the last two beads picked up (**f–g**).

Row 14: Pick up five beads, and loop around row 13 as shown (**g–h**). *Pick

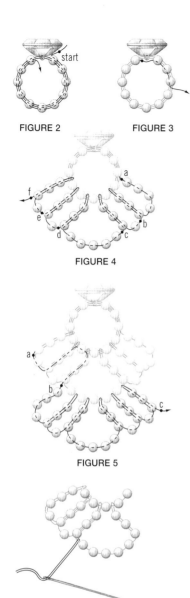

FIGURE 2   FIGURE 3

FIGURE 4

FIGURE 5

FIGURE 6

Follow the pattern shown for the last row. Note that you go back through two beads instead of one after connecting to the three-bead groups.

Finishing
[1] Tie an overhand knot with the pair of base cords against the last bead on the left of the base row. Tie the end of the base cords together with an overhand knot, and tie another knot about ½ in. (1.3cm) closer to the necklace.
[2] Insert a pencil between the two end knots, and twist the cords until they begin to fold back on themselves.
[3] Wet thoroughly, then press with a steam iron under a presscloth to make the twists permanent.
[4] Repeat at the other end. Trim off the final end knots.

Ecuadorian leaf bracelet
This bracelet is made with a single repeating unit, which is a modified form of Saraguro netting that produces a lacy fabric. Each consecutive unit builds upon the previous one. The bracelets shown below are made with both triangle beads and seed beads. The figures show the bracelet worked in two colors, but it also looks beautiful in a single color.
[1] Center a needle on about 2 yd. (1.8m) of conditioned Nymo.
[2] Working with doubled thread, pick up 11 color A beads and the button or clasp, leaving a 4-in. (10cm) tail. Go back through all the beads and the clasp to form a circle. Go through all the beads a third time, but don't go through the clasp (**figure 2**).
[3] Skip the button, and go through the next three beads (**figure 3**). This is the base of the first unit.
[4] Complete the unit as shown in **figure 4**: Pick up seven color B beads, skip a base bead, loop around the thread, and go back through the last three beads pick up (**a–b**).

Pick up one B and three As, skip a base bead, loop around the thread, and go back through the last three beads picked up (**b–c**).

Pick up eight As, skip a base bead, loop around the thread, and go back through the last three beads picked up (**c–d**). Note that the first five beads form the base for the next unit.

Pick up four Bs, skip a base bead, loop around the thread, and go back through the last three beads picked up (**d–e**).

Pick up four Bs, skip a base bead, loop around the thread, and go back through the last three beads picked up (**e–f**).
[5] Backtrack through the last two loops as shown in **figure 5, a–b**. Work the next unit as you did the first one, using the five center beads of the previous unit as the new base (**b–c**).
[6] To add thread, weave the short tail back through the last two loops as you would to end a unit, making a few half-hitch knots (Techniques) between beads, and trim the tail close to the beadwork. To begin a new double thread, center the new thread on the center loop where the thread would normally start, and thread both ends into the needle (**figure 6**). Resume beading.
[7] When you get to the last unit, instead of picking up eight beads in the center loop, pick up enough beads to fit around the button. If you used a clasp instead of a button, pick up two beads, the ring of the clasp, and five more beads. In either case, finish the unit. Weave in the tail securely, and retrace the thread path of the large center loop. Tie two or three half-hitch knots, and trim. Secure the beginning tail the same way.

CONTRIBUTORS

Dorothy Bonitz began making French beaded flowers some fifty years ago and takes pride in designing each beaded flower piece to look botanically correct. Contact her at (276) 930-1809 or rosemary@swva.com.

Karin Buckingham is a jewelry designer and former Associate Editor of *BeadStyle*. Contact her in care of Kalmbach Books.

Jennifer Creasey is a jewelry designer and bead artist whose work is featured on the Web site polarbeads.com.

Anna Elizabeth Draeger is an Associate Editor at *Bead&Button* magazine. Contact her in care of *Bead&Button*.

Karen Frankfeldt teaches beading classes in the New York City area. Contact her at Karen@blbglaw.com

Julia Gerlach is an Associate Editor at *Bead&Button* magazine. Contact her in care of *Bead&Button*.

Gloria Harris is a retired teacher who travels and beads. Contact her in care of Kalmbach Books.

Mindi Hawman's beadwork has appeared in *Bead&Button*. Contact her in care of Kalmbach Books.

Susan Hillyer has contributed to *Bead&Button*. Contact her in care of Kalmbach Books.

Ella Johnson-Bentley's love of beading began almost twenty years ago. She teaches beading classes in Alaska, Ore., and at the *Bead&Button* Show. Contact her at ella@gci.net.

Alice Korach was the founding editor of *Bead&Button*. Visit her Web site lostwaxglass.com.

Heidi Kummli is an award-winning bead embroidery artist. See her designs at freespiritcollection.com.

Sarah Ladiges is an owner of the Bead Hut, in Kirkland, Wash. Contact her at (425) 827-6286.

Misty Leppard is an artist and teacher of bead weaving and polymer clay. She also works in PMC and fused glass and shows her work in galleries and fairs. Contact her at mistyleppard@msn.com.

Kelly Lightner's beadwork has appeared in *Bead&Button*. Contact her through Kalmbach Books.

Tracy List has been making lamp-worked beads and jewelry for eight years, occasionally teaching classes and selling her jewelry at local shows in Farmington, Calif. View her work at elmstreetcreations.com and contact her through the Web site.

April Machan owns Ruby Dragon Designs in Waterford, Wis. Contact her at amachan@hotmail.com; subject: Ruby Dragon Designs.

Kate McKinnon is a prolific bead artist and jewelry designer. See her work at katemckinnon.com. E-mail her at kate@katemckinnon.com.

Judy Mullins is a beadwork artist from Tigard, Ore. Contact her at bead.garden@verizon.net.

Lea Nowicki is a frequent contributor to *Bead&Button* and *BeadStyle* magazines. Contact her in care of Kalmbach books.

Bonnie O'Donnell-Painter can be reached at cubuffnut@aol.com.

Rebecca Peapples has been beading for 25 years. E-mail her at RSPeapples@aol.com.

Sonja Podjan has been doing beadwork for 14 years. She is the author of three beading books. See her work at angelfire.com/mi/beadsgalore or contact her at slpodjan@cpuinc.net.

Carol Pulk is a jewelry designer and cancer survivor who beads to stay actively creative. A graduate of the Fashion Institute of Technology in New York City, Carol can be reached at carolandchloe@alltel.net.

Kathy Rice's work has been featured in *Bead&Button*. Contact her in care of Kalmbach Books.

Mary Anne Russell's beadwork has appeared in *Bead&Button*. Contact her through Kalmbach Books.

Beth Ruth offers the jump ring bracelet as a kit. Contact her at Acme Bead Company, 41 W. Maple St., Sturgeon Bay, WI 54235; (920) 559-7446 or visit her Web site, acmebeadcompany.com

Rebecca Starry can be reached at (907) 269-6297 or via e-mail at instig8r@alaska.net.

Siobhan Sullivan's beadwork is featured on her Web site, queenofbeading.com. Contact her through her Web site or via e-mail at siobhans@optonline.net.

Lila Tubbs's peyote pattern has appeared in *Bead&Button*. Contact her in care of Kalmbach Books.

Lesley Weiss is an Assistant Editor at Kalmbach Books. Contact her in care of Kalmbach Books.

Nancy Zellers is a bead artist and teacher in Colorado. She exhibits frequently in local and national shows. Contact her at nzbeads@aol.com.

INDEX